# building brand YOU!

# building brand YOU!

## Essentials for Corporate Success

Mamata R Talukdar
Sanjiv S Chaudhary

RUPA
PUBLICATIONS INDIA

Published 2012 by
**Rupa Publications India Pvt. Ltd.**
7/16, Ansari Road, Daryaganj,
New Delhi 110 002

*Sales Centres:*

Allahabad Bengaluru Chennai
Hyderabad Jaipur Kathmandu
Kolkata Mumbai



Printed in India by
Nutech Photolithographers
B-240, Okhla Industrial Area, Phase-I,
New Delhi 110 020

*To Deti and Ma*

*For bringing me into this world and providing me with abundant physical, emotional, psychological and intellectual nourishment.*

– Mamata R Talukdar

*To my Daddy, Late Shree Sohan Lal,*
*Though you did not live long with us, you were always present to guide us and make us better human beings.*
*Thank you 'Daddy'.*

– Sanjiv S Chaudhary

# CONTENTS

# PREFACE

It is a fact that opinions are formed about you just about anywhere in the professional world – in meetings, reviews, corridors and corners. As a professional, you are constantly gauged according to your attitude, intelligence and personality. You are being judged and evaluated by everybody around you – in every gesture or reaction in any situation, your behaviour with fellow associates, during official reviews, during casual conversations, while working in a group, and random discussions.

Each one of us desire to be known as dependable, diligent, dedicated, intelligent, sincere and as overall good professionals and human beings. We are all ambitious and we all dream of being successful, no matter what profession we are in. To get into your desired profession you need to develop knowledge and skills of that profession. More importantly, to grow in that profession, you need to gain a name for yourself and also a fan following, whether in your own team, by peers in your organisation or in the industry. Combination of knowledge and attitude leaves an everlasting impact on people around you and that is what is called 'impression'. This book is all about creating the right impression through gesture and action.

When someone has to give an opinion about you, you would certainly desire to have given a positive impression. But, these positive words don't come so easily. They are earned over a period of time and with your constant endeavour to create a good impression. We take days and years to create such impressions knowingly and unknowingly. But, mind you, you may shatter the same in no time at all.

As Warren Buffet had stated:

> It takes twenty years to build a reputation and five
> minutes to ruin it. If you think about that,
> you'll do things differently.

It may sound difficult to keep everyone happy and to ensure that everyone carries a good impression about you. But doing things in the right perspective with good intentions is all one needs to focus on. Everyone wants to grow in the professional sphere and would like to access the right opportunity at the right time. Today most organisations fill almost 90 per cent of vacancies through references. And only the person who carries a good opinion of you will refer you. And this starts as early as from your college times. Your network spreads across through your colleagues, friends, peers, relatives, teachers, mentors, trainers, etc. This in turn provides you with chances to gain more and more opportunities, and hence lead to growth.

There is a famous Chinese proverb:

> Make happy those who are near,
> and those who are far will come.

It is believed that a good balance of intelligence and attitude is a sure-shot way to success in the corporate world. As you go up the corporate ladder, it is your attitude and intelligence, put together, that carries you to the pinnacle of success. It has been observed that if it is your intelligence that ignites your career, it is definitely your attitude which accelerates it at a much faster pace. On the matrix of intelligence and attitude, if you are high on intelligence and low on attitude, it ensures success up to an extent but certainly does not make you a leader. However, if you are high on attitude, it ensures long and steady success. And moreover, attitude cultivates an intelligent atmosphere and attracts followers, and makes a professional a good leader and a better manager. Attitude has the potential to manage intelligence and to help one lead with success.

This brings us to the question – what is attitude? Attitude, as a definition would have different versions described by many in their own way. Attitude is to do with your behaviour, gestures, your reaction and actions in a situation, the words you choose to use, your body language, your dealings, etc. When we say 'situation' it would mean any situation, whether you are working alone, presenting your performance, sharing your views, taking reviews, walking down the corridor, travelling with your seniors, dropping your colleague at home, standing with colleagues in elevators and so on. You are being observed and judged for your behaviour, gestures and reactions and this plays a major part in defining your attitude. If you want to know about your attitude, notice yourself when you are alone. Note what you think and how you react in certain situations or to people, what are the thoughts running in your mind. That is your real attitude. It is almost impossible to be dishonest to yourself. If you are generous and humane, kind words or ways to improve relationships are the first thoughts that would occur to you; you will notice the brighter and better side of people and situations. If you are the vengeful kind, you will catch yourself finding ways to make people feel low, words you use will invariably lead towards revenge. These give insight into your attitude.

A student spends year after year studying books, magazines, making projects, trying to gather more knowledge about their core subject to learn and improve their thinking ability; but they often seem to miss building the softer aspects and interpersonal skills – in building the right attitude!

This is what we find lacking in our educational system. One is expected to learn through self-education. But more often than not, a student already loses out on his/her precious years by learning through trial and error. In recent times, our educational institutes are finding a need for business schools to devote time to look at personality development, business and personal communication skills, and overall etiquette for managers to operate successfully in today's complex environments. There is a global need today for course correction to create graduates who are effective from day one. Our courses are too scientific and research-oriented; professors have limited real world experience and students who graduate end up ill-equipped to wrangle with complex issues and ethics. So one can now see a paradigm shift in these courses with a sharper focus on soft skill development pertaining to people management, understanding social contexts and effective communication.

More and more corporates today are looking for people who have the attitude to deal with competitive situations. Not only in the corporate world but also in your personal world - if you are someone who is intelligent and fun to be with, well mannered, polite, polished - people like to be seen around you. No one likes to be seen with someone sloppy. As a family person you have to be a father/mother, brother/sister, wife/husband, daughter/son and you are expected to fulfil all the roles with equal attention. The corporate world is also made of real people and hence expectations are the same.

Our book revolves around all the possible situations which any working professional would come across throughout his career. Each situation is an occasion to form an opinion. You may not be able to build a fabulous impression in one interaction. However, you risk losing your impression in just one instance, if you have failed to give it appropriate attention. An impression once broken is difficult to rebuild. It may take double the effort to rebuild it or you may not get a chance to rebuild at all.

Everyone is ambitious and works hard with the right intention in mind. Professionals do make mistakes but mostly do so unknowingly. What one must keep in mind is that nobody tells you about your bad habits or about issues like bad breath. Self-education is learning through your experiences and situations. But a little bit of guidance will go a long way in your journey of self-education and will save you many precious years. This book will guide you in a practical way to constantly make a good impression in most instances of the corporate world and would also empower you to develop your own sensitivities to deal with situations that are not covered in this book. It will certainly make you conscious enough to use common sense to help you deal with any situation in the best possible way. It will create an awareness of the importance of making a good impression and having the right attitude in your life and career. Impression is the 'S' of your success, if you adopt it at an early stage in your career you have started spelling your success, but if you ignore it, you have to make double the effort to regain the last 'ss'.

If you have bought this book and have read this far, we can assure you that you are headed in the right direction of awareness and implementation.

## How We Wrote this Book

This book is written from what we have seen, heard and most importantly experienced through our lives in the corporate world. We have made mistakes, observed the attitude of seniors and peers, noticed whose attitude is seemingly more pleasant and learnt to build our attitude the hard way. We did take to reading books, but could not find anything that could help us in the practical world. Firstly, everything was Western; secondly, it is so much theory and *gyaan* that if we go to apply all of that in our lives, it actually looks very artificial. We can assure you, these are tips from real-life experiences which we have gathered by being in the corporate world over the years, and we have been put through the grind and learnt things the hard way – by trial and error. One thing we have realised beyond doubt is that WE ARE CONSTANTLY UNDER THE RADAR, we are being observed intentionally and unintentionally by seniors, peers, and team members.

Our book brings you insights from the real world. There's no theory – only practical experiences and how we have combated the corporate world, giving you the finer details so that you gain your success at a much faster pace and you do not make simple and silly mistakes, to build an everlasting impression.

**Why this Book?**

As you read on you will notice we don't expect you to keep a note on things like body posture. Some of the books we have read are written with so much detail and explanation that it weighs heavily on one's head. You tend to get confused on what is of absolute importance and what is not. What are those things which you have some more time to cultivate, which are not posing a disaster to your career growth right at this moment; and what are the things that you must change or incorporate into your life immediately, which otherwise would spell disaster to your career growth. There's so much written about that perfect handshake. What we would think works is – you should look straight into the eyes of the person on the other side and give him/her a firm handshake and not a limp one. THAT'S IT! Bothering about the thumb being in a particular position, and the forefinger here and the little finger there, is not something we could possibly remember, or even care to bother about. If the person on the other side is really following 'all the rules of the perfect handshake' or not, it would definitely not make someone form 'an opinion' about him/her. But yes, if the handshake was limp and the person was looking here and there and not into your eyes, you would think, why is s/he not confident enough to hold my hand and shake it right?

Sad but true, perception rules the corporate world, so to be able to create 'that' impression you have to bear with some of this.

## Market Yourself

'Market yourself'. You are a brand. You are a commodity waiting to develop as a branded product. You have to market yourself. Brands are earned; you as a branded product have to demonstrate your competitive edge. To earn respect you need to make sure people follow you, are loyal to you. To make people follow you, you have to lead by demonstration and you have to demonstrate well. This book puts you in the path of demonstrating good manners and etiquette in every aspect of your professional life. However, brands are not built overnight, but their journey and how long they will survive is indicated from the beginning.

Remember, the first relationship with anyone as a professional is of work. Work should be carried out with sincerity and dedication. But this book does not attempt to teach you that. In fact we doubt any book can teach you about that. But what this book will teach you is how to be disciplined to do that work. And, both are equally important. What we do, how we do it, what we say, builds our impression and the other person starts to sketch a portrait of us in his mind. Actually what s/he has drawn in his/her mind, we ourselves have portrayed it. Whether the brand looks good or ugly, it is only because of us. And our book would help you do just that. Build your brand!

**Who is this Book for?**

This book is specifically for the young professional and entrepreneurs from any industry, expatriates working Indian assignments and students of all institutions specialising in any field, who will be joining this corporate world. It is also recommended for senior level executives. Not only will it help them brush up their skills but it may also be helpful to share tips with one's team if one is convinced about these aspects and believes in building a professional culture and learning in one's team and organisation. We believe these attributes are learnt through experimentation and with experience. We make mistakes and learn from them (ideally) but there may be times we may not even know of our mistakes and keep making the same mistake unknowingly till we find that it is too late. If this book reaches out to more and more professionals like you, our purpose of impacting that aspect of your career will be successful. May we all grow successful together.

This book is written with an objective to ensure a position in every home library. When in a tricky situation, you may refer to this book. For a new reader not used to reading a number of pages at a stretch, we have further categorised our longer sessions into smaller sections. You may note your reading habits and space out this book for reading at your convenience. In fact, if you are not a reader already, this book might also help you start a habit of reading.

This book is written in simple language. Have you come across any word or sentence so far that you haven't understood? The entire book is written like this, such that it will help you enhance your speed of reading. The scope of this book revolves around your inner beauty and very practical aspects of your attitude. All the learnings and insights from here can be directed towards building the right attitude, which is as important as developing your core competencies.

This book promises you no gyaan. The gyaan session was just till here to reach a common understanding between you, the reader, and us, the writers. From the first session itself, we promise practical attributes which you can use in a day-to-day professional world. You need to wake up now! Act now! In today's competitive world and on a fast-paced race to success, fame, respect, self-esteem, satisfaction, power and position, we cannot afford to leave it to chance!!

Let's begin with session one! We have ten sessions; all of them are equally important and interesting. The first session is communication. To know why this session is the first session, let's go further and understand.

# ACKNOWLEDGEMENTS

My first thanks goes to my co-writer Sanjiv. Thank you for your belief in me and having faith that I could partner you to give your concept the shape of a book. Had you not initiated it I perhaps would have never attempted to write a book.

Rupa Publications, my publisher and my editor Suzanne Hughe, for considering our book worth publishing and providing immense support thereafter. I have been writing a bit since childhood but never thought I could write something that someone would pay to read, or even read for free. You made me believe that I could.

Thanks to all my wonderful ex-bosses and colleagues under whose guidance/influence I have flourished as a professional. Without those years with you all I could never have attempted to write this book. I remembered all of you while writing it.

Spriha, my little one. Thank you for tolerating my absence while I was away at work, and then coming back home to my laptop again, to write this book.

Last but definitely not the least is the person who has maximum influence in my life, who I have practically grown up with, my love, my friend, my husband, my father figure – Raja. I am because of you!

Mamata R Talukdar

# ACKNOWLEDGEMENTS

Every dream is a thought and to transform that thought into reality requires inspiration, support and the love of people around you. I have been fortunate enough to have such beautiful people around me with their blind trust, unconditional support and silent prayers.

With folded hands I bow my head, first and foremost, to Maa. I offer my deepest thanks to you, for our wonderful upbringing. Losing our dad at such an early age, you did not let us fall short of anything we desired to have as kids or adults. Your courage to face the world alone and ability to give love and blessings with open hands has always been a matter of pride for us. We owe to you where we are today and we dedicate to you where we will be tomorrow. Thank you Maa!

For me you have been a father figure and one of the finest human beings I have in my life. Your ability to take pain and sorrow and filter happiness in every regard to everyone in the family has been instrumental in making all our dreams come true. With my heartfelt deep regards I owe every second of my life to these remarkable humans, my elder brother Satish and Kusum bhabhi. Thank you Bhabhi and Paaji!

Before I thank my sweetheart, Monika, I would like to thank Mrs and Lt. Col. Arjun Singh Manhas for giving me a piece of their heart, which is full of kindness, intelligence, exemplary honesty and simplicity just like you. I wish to tell the world, each second of encouragement and your unrelenting support has made this book possible. Monika, love you!

Karina and Sankalp my niece and nephew, Saundarya and Angel my darling daughters, you all are our inspirations; a smile from you is worth endless wealth. Keep smiling ... always. Bless you!!

I believe that no two people meet without any purpose. The association with Mamata has resulted in us developing our thoughts in the form of this book and hopefully more to come. Mamata, your intelligence, maturity and adaptability is remarkable. Thank you for everything.

Last but not the least, thanks to each one of you who have inadvertently reinforced our thoughts to give our concept the shape of a book!!

Enjoy.

Sanjiv S Chaudhary

"Communication in the corporate world is like a family function at home.
It is the type of function which decides whom to communicate with and how much."

# Session I

# COMMUNICATION

First of all, most of us will pronounce this word wrong. Just read again, you might have pronounced 'KO-mu-nee-kay-shun', right? If yes, it is not your fault; English as a language is intricate and at times utterly confusing. There are so many words which you might end up pronouncing, by stitching together the letters and vowels. So it is important that wherever and whenever you get a chance to learn the right pronunciation, do not miss it. If you happen to have studied in a good convent school and even more importantly under a good teacher, pronunciation by now will come naturally to you. But most of us are not so fortunate!

One of the advantages of globalisation is that BPOs/call centres/service centres are located in different parts of the world. For many businesses it is quite important, rather compulsory, to pick the right pronunciation and modulation of words.

English as a language is divided broadly in two dialects and modulation, British and American. Most of you would be travelling the world and will meet people from different parts of the world. Picking up the right pronunciation of words is extremely important. Getting it right the first time not only draws the attention of your listeners, but also creates a good impression on the other side. Do not leave any opportunity to pick up the right pronunciation of words.

The word 'communication' is spoken as 'k-mu-nee-kay-shun' not 'ko' but only 'k'. Most of us shape our lips round and make the sound 'ko'. Figure out how pronunciations work there are several books on it, you will enjoy learning it.

Communication is what you speak and write – this could be the simplest definition of the word. However, there is a little bit more to communication than merely the words you use to put forward your thoughts and opinion. There is a finer detail to communication which most of us miss out on, and that is the INTENT! Appropriate words used, with the right intent, would build your character and the way people view you. What we mean by intent will be taken up during the course of the session.

This is your first impression. A lot of thought has gone into figuring out what builds the first and most lasting impression. And we unanimously decided, it's none other than communication, hence this comes to you as your first session. You might have noticed, in your life, whatever you do and wherever you are, even before you speak there are some other aspects that build your first impression. Those are your accessories and appearance. Keeping this in mind, appearance should have been the first session, isn't it? Well, no! Not now in today's world of communication. Today, technology takes you places where even your appearance and accessories have not reached.

Let's take an example. Today you write an email to a group of people, when half of your colleagues have not seen you, but only read you. Even if they have spoken to you over the phone, they have only heard your speaking style and pronunciation, and the words you choose. Similarly, your teams across states and nations have already made their impression about you, before meeting you in person.

There could be a number of examples, but let's just stick to the one we picked. Take for example this book. You gather an impression of us by reading this book, even before we actually meet. Give it a thought – you will be able to visualise how these days technology carries your impression and your style of business culture, and even you as a person!

In any situation in your business world and profession, there is verbal and non-verbal communication. In this session we will be covering both verbal communication and non-verbal communication. Keep this in mind, even silence speaks. It forms an extremely important aspect of your personality.

So we see we have been able to hold your interest long enough for you to get here. Let us promise you one thing – it's only going to get better! Let's do some serious reading now.

Let's start by breaking this topic into two parts, just to ensure we do not miss out on any topic/situation.

- Written
- Spoken

Before we focus on the 'spoken' we will discuss the 'written' aspect of communication, as we are going in a sequence and as mentioned earlier, the written word has the ability to spread like a forest fire, a virus and even fragrance – it has the power to create both positive and negative impressions in equal strength. Had this book been written a couple of years back, the sequence would probably have been different. But we think, in a real sense the way of communicating has changed, and so has the priority.

## WRITTEN

The moment you read 'written', could you wrap your brain around it? What comes under this subject?

**Email**

Electronic mail has had an electrifying effect on business. In a typical working day, a person on an average spends almost 30 per cent to 40 per cent of their time on email. Reading, writing, replying, forwarding, follow-ups, taking action based on mails, etc. Almost half of your day is consumed thus, so imagine how much discipline is warranted and how organised you ought to be. Most of the time, your day is planned based on your mails, sometime it interrupts your routine and many a time reminds you about important tasks and puts you on track to help you plan your day. Email is one of the most powerful tools today, and can be used both constructively and destructively. Right now we stick to 'CONTENT'. We have come across many occasions when office email is down and both the business and the office come to a standstill. Soon the entire office has a holiday mood. Well, that's another opportunity for you to make an impression and another situation to deal with – leisure time in office. We will discuss 'LEISURE' at a later time. Meanwhile, let's dissect 'email' for a better understanding of it.

## Subject of the Email

The subject of the mail will attract recipients to read it. Be sure your subject is in line with the objective of your mail.

The subject should not be more than four words. Do not make it a sentence. While writing to your seniors and professional business partners, do not use any symbols or signs like exclamations or question marks, unless it is mandatory. It's okay to use these characters with mail forwards amongst friends, not official mail.

Avoid writing the subject in capital letters (other than abbreviation). Letters written in capital are understood as yelling and shouting.

If you are forwarding any mail, where you do not want the trail mail to be forwarded, ensure that the word 'Fwd:' is also deleted. Imagine what the receiver might perceive from this otherwise – that you may be hiding something and this makes a bad impression for sure; even your intention would be questioned.

Under any circumstances, a mail should not leave your outbox without a subject. In case you receive a forwarded mail where your colleague has forgotten to mention the subject, add a suitable subject before forwarding the mail further.

You could be casual in writing the subject of a mail in your friend circle. But you need to use caution in official mails.

### Golden Tip

Never ever write a mail when you are riding high on emotions, or when you are at your wits' end. Always take that extra time to cool down before clicking on that send button – else the repercussions may be disastrous!

**Addressing the Recipient of an Email**

'Respected', 'Mr', 'Madam', 'Sir', are the salutations that come to our mind as we think of addressing someone senior. And there is no harm in accepting or being proud that we have grown up in a culture where till just a couple of years back, we could not even imagine addressing someone senior without 'Sir' or 'Madam'. But things are different now. During Sanjiv's study abroad, way back in 1995, a twenty-six-year-old student was expected to call a sixty-year-old teacher by first name. This was a culture shock for all students coming from a conservative society.

But today, with the new generation growing to higher levels and a change in people's mindset to accept and adopt this transformation, the scenario has changed rather drastically.

Today, nobody minds being called by their first name, especially in the professional world. This happens not only in the corporate world. In fact in the school Mamata's daughter goes to, the students address their principal and teachers by their first name. But this change is yet to be accepted and adopted in the social world. For example, you still cannot call your mother-in-law by her first name (and we're happy to call her 'Ma'). Globalisation has happened due to business collaborations, and hence a global culture has already seeped into all business transactions. There is still time for social collaborations!

Addressing a person in an official mail by saying 'Hi' and 'Hey' is unprofessional as they are considered slang. But of course 'Hi' is quite acceptable among peers and even members who are part of your team.

So you see, you needn't use salutations like Respected, Sir, etc., to your seniors in office. Now everybody accepts being addressed by first name. Use a salutation like 'Dear All' when you have to address more than one person and while addressing one person 'Dear Alok' is quite acceptable. By the way, addressing somebody by first name does not mean s/he has not been respected. It all depends on how the body of the email is structured after the address. And by all means avoid calling anyone 'uncle' or 'aunty' in office even if you know them personally or otherwise.

**Body of the Email**

Typically like in a letter, if you are initiating a mail, you divide the body into three parts.

1. Reference with objective of the mail
2. Description/update of the objective
3. A thank-you note.

In business communication you do not write as you speak. Ensure sentences are phrased in business language. Do not write long sentences and very lengthy mails. Some people have this habit of writing lengthy mails. Over a period of time they are either ignored or become a laughing stock. Their mails lose all attraction and more importantly, the IMPACT. Just in case you have to, break the body into reference points (like we have done above while describing the body of the mail) rather than sentences, so it is easy for receivers to skim through the mail and get into the details of only what is relevant to them. Most of us prefer to skim through mails, and try and gather the objective or abstract of it. Hence, to get the 'punch' in your mails, make it brief, make it relevant, break it up into reference points and outline well.

Most organisations have a brand font and prefer their employees to use that font. Be disciplined and use brand font and size. This is one way of showing respect to the organisation and love for your brand. But in case your organisation does not have this as a policy, pick one which is widely acceptable and that you like. Ensure the one you pick is widely acceptable and does not become an obstacle in the reading flow and speed of the readers. For example, Times New Roman is quite reader friendly. A good font not only enhances the speed of reading, but also keeps the reader calm and able to concentrate on the content of the mail. So, select a cool font for yourself and let that be your font. You too are an upcoming brand as you are finishing this book. Start making your own style statements.

Using difficult English words is not a matter of pride. Your idea of sending mail is for people to read and act on it. If your vocabulary comes in the way of your achieving that, it's of no use. You should write what is easy to read and easily understandable. Today you have the choice to right-click and choose any word, but do pick the simple ones.

Highlighting in different colours and using a bigger font is not appreciated. Your creativity may be looked upon by business people as frivolous and immature, rather than them appreciating you for it. Be very choosy in picking your words. Ensure you are polite and within your protocol in choosing words. 'Kindly', 'please', 'allow me', 'thank you', 'apology', 'appreciate' are not just words, these convey your attitude.

## Intent of the Email

You ought to be sensitive about who you are marking a mail to. Marking mails to people who are unrelated or even only remotely related to that topic, creates a very damaging impression about the person sending it.

Using mail as a means to get work done may not go down too well with your colleagues, especially if you are escalating an issue with their bosses. They might find it intimidating. It works better to have a couple of rounds of discussion – reminding one another about it casually while crossing each other in the corridors or while in the lunch room or through phone calls. Even after all of this, if the work is not done, then of course we know the intention of our co-worker – s/he is in no mood to get the work done (for whatever reason), then by all means escalate. Otherwise, a mail should be restricted to passing information, summarising discussions, sharing Minutes of Meeting (MOM), sharing action plan with timelines, etc.

### Golden rule

Using email as an escalation tool is again an art. Escalating to the right people and at the right time is important. You may escalate to the next level if the recipient has not reverted back to you within the turnaround time. Then we give some more time for them to revert depending on the criticality of the topic. However, like we have mentioned above, it is suggested to always give a couple of calls, or walk down to the desk of the person you are expecting a revert from, and post that if you still do not get a revert, that you will go ahead and escalate.

Escalation in the corporate world is an art/skill you are expected to pick up early. Whom to escalate to, when to escalate and how to escalate and most importantly, what to escalate defines your attention, sincerity, and sensitivity to issues and concerns. There are issues which require escalation within seconds and some others that can wait some more time, depending on the sensitivity of the issue. Take a simple example of social escalation. What will you do when somebody has met with an accident, and got only minor bruises? Who will you inform and how? Similarly, if some close relative has expired in the accident (god forbid), who will you inform and how? Professional escalations are all about alerting seniors or people concerned about sensitive issues like accidents and causalities of your work; and professional escalation is also all about informing the right person, at the right time, with the right information. Think about a birthday celebration and a wedding ceremony. We are sure your list of invitees for the birthday and the wedding ceremony will differ. A similar process of elimination or inclusion should be used while sending a mail for, say, a small process change note vis-á-vis sending a mail for a product launch. One of the most important principles of management is escalation. The earlier you learn, the better the pace you set for yourself for growth.

If you wish to spread a word of appreciation then it is always suggested to mark it to the bosses. But please do not mark a 'thank you' mail to ALL marked in CC. That not only occupies unnecessary space in everybody's inbox, but is also seen as a very casual attitude (which is not appreciated in the corporate world) on your part.

## Ending an Email

As we have understood and recommended – mail should be crisp and short unless you are sending a detailed action plan. In any scenario, a similar rule will apply for OUTLINING.

The ending of the mail should not exceed more than one or two sentences. It's a human tendency to be in a hurry, or for any reader in an office atmosphere. You might have lost the attention of your reader as s/he approaches the end of the mail. But your objective is to ensure your reader gives due attention to the expectations from your mail, and ensure that you get a response. So the ending should clearly state your expectations only and not the summary of your body again. Words like 'appreciate help', 'please support', etc., reflect team building and a good attitude, and helps you bond with people.

It is fair to give timelines to your peers and juniors (not recommended for your seniors) with direct guidelines. You can convey your expectations and urgency to your seniors indirectly, e.g. mention by when you expect yourself to finish this activity, what support you would require from your senior to do so, etc. There is also no harm walking down to your boss and reminding him/her. Even otherwise it's a good idea to show your boss your face once in a while; it does have its long-term benefits. Even a boss is human; s/he will keep in mind that you keep note of your responsibilities.

Signing off as 'Yours truly' or 'Yours sincerely', etc., are things of the past. 'Regards' or 'Thanks & regards' work well enough. Even to very senior people.

**Signature**

It is recommended that you provide your details at the end of the mail. You never know how far and wide your mail is going to travel, and what shape your mail takes. Do not give anyone a chance to ask – 'Who is the person who has initiated this communication?'. It reflects badly on you and makes you look careless.

Most organisations have certain policies and guidelines on uniform signature patterns. But the execution of these policies lies with you. Do not ignore this. It shows disrespect for your organisation guidelines. If there are no guidelines provided, you may go ahead and set your own. Lead the pack and others will follow you. Let's give you an idea of what a good signature looks like.

**<your name>|<role>|<function>|<contact details>**
**<Address>**
**<Company logo> <Team log>**
**<Tag along>**

Your signature must have your name, your function, the role you are handling and your designation. Adding on your company logo/team logo, company punchline, etc., demonstrates your pride and loyalty to the company. What is important is your role or the position that you are answerable for. Provide full details of your office address and your contact numbers. Generally, women may want to avoid publishing their numbers to avoid blank and prank calls, but do mention your office numbers. All mail applications have a feature of 'by default' signature.

Setting it up as default makes your job easy. Be disciplined in your signature. It speaks for you.

Your signature gives you another opportunity to display what you believe in, and that helps depict your personality – attaching a 'tag along'. A good quotation or messages on a social cause or seasonal greetings are some examples. This not only makes your signature interesting, but also you as a person. We recommend taking time out to refresh your 'tag along' once a week or a fortnight. You may add a message on social and environmental causes like 'Go Green', or 'Save paper'. But do write what you truly believe in. Over a period of time you will realise your peers like to read your mail and look forward to the 'tag along'.

By the way, adding phrases from this book as your 'tag along' is a good idea. You will be instrumental in bringing about a change in your friends' or colleagues' career and life.

### Forwarding an Email

Forwarding mail without your comment/synopsis with FYI (For Your Information) remarks is seen as rude and is a bad reflection of your attitude. Adding a line of the objective of the trail mail is always appreciated. Outlined conclusion and synopsis of the mail is welcome by any receiver. Forwarding to seniors with a simple FYI may prove absolutely disastrous.

### Replying to an Email

The most important part of emailing is to reply within an acceptable time. It is, in fact, one of the most important responsibilities of your job. Getting a reminder should be treated as highly inefficient on your part; because the rest of the world would certainly view it as such. Maximum work is via mail in today's world. Either we are initiating a mail or replying to a mail. Like you would expect a timely response to your mails, so also the others have the same expectation from you; which is a rightful expectation. A whole lot of work goes behind responding to a mail, so you must ensure you start working behind the scene as soon as you receive a mail that demands your response. Also, promise a TAT (Turn Around Time) to a mail after giving due consideration to the amount of work you yourself have to put in and also giving reasonable time to others, whose support you would require, to send a smart response. Responding on time will always stand by you; it will never let you down. You might not immediately have the required knowledge or information and need more time to respond, even then make it a point to place the same on mail. If you aren't able to get back within the TAT you have committed, please drop in a line apologising and providing a new TAT. Here it also helps if you can give a quick overview of the status as of that day. Leaving any mail unattended and transferring it to your folder without replying is a crime. Please do not commit this crime.

All applications come with up-to-date features of setting follow-ups, etc., to help you efficiently manage your work and mails. We would advise you to make the best use of technology and use these applications to the optimum. Good knowledge about these applications also creates a cool impression.

## Email Etiquettes

'To' should be only marked to the person from whom you expect a reply. Keeping more than one name in 'To' might not get the desired response, as per your expectation. One cannot deny this human tendency to pass the buck on to another person, so it is better to keep one person in 'To', so as to place ownership on one person who would be left with no other choice but to take it upon him or herself to respond to you. If the job requires equal attention of two or more people, then use the body of the mail to segregate the responsibilities along with the owners for each responsibility.

Do not mark all emails to seniors unless important. Only escalations should be marked to them. This brings us to the topic that we touched upon a while back, INTENT. Please refer to that session as this is the most sensitive part of emailing etiquette.

## Non-Official Emails

Fun forwards should be sent to your friends' circle only, unless you are otherwise friendly with your bosses. Here again, do not attempt to build a friendship by forwarding jokes, etc., to seniors. You have to build that relationship first. Forwarding emails should only be a by-product of your already existing friendship, and are not to be used as a tool to create that 'friendship'. You would be seen as trying to be over-friendly. For example, forwarding a mail to your boss where you are comparing bosses with pigs, or any such email, will never be appreciated by any boss.

Even among friends and peers, do not blindly mark emails to groups. Over a period of time you will be seen as a pest and no matter how impacting or interesting your mail forwards are, it would be looked upon as a disturbance. If you forward with caution, you will elevate your respect among friends and colleagues. Do share a forward once in a while, else you will be seen as an 'all work and no play' person. Striking a balance has always been the key in whatever you do, you would agree, right? Hence, something as simple as forwarding mails also needs that much attention. We wonder why some of us get ahead at a much faster pace, while some of us get left behind. What is it that they do differently to accelerate their growth? You do the same amount of work, with the same seriousness and commitment (maybe more sometimes), yet you feel you have been surpassed by some. These are the little things we fail to pay attention to, and thus fail to create that impression which will portray us as ready for the next level. These seemingly small things spell your maturity.

**Respect Privacy**

Do not read anyone's mailbox, unless the person asks you to. It is extremely poor on your part to stare at the screen of your colleague without any reason. No one would mention it, but it stays in a person's mind that you are someone one has to be cautious of. You will be viewed with suspicion and as an intruder in someone else's life. Sometimes the person whose screen you are peeping into may change the face of the screen ... imagine what an embarrassing moment that would be for you. So you better not give anyone a chance to embarrass you. We are trying to build this really suave and well-mannered professional through this book; all the work you have put in to read the book so far, and the hard work we have put in to write this book for you, would go down the drain because of such a small little gaffe. So let's work together to build you up into this most desirable professional.

### Some Quick Fixes

Keep your mailbox maintained as per your email box limit. Bouncing emails at regular intervals reflects an unplanned and casual approach.

Do not get personal in your email. In case you want to highlight an issue, by all means do so, but don't highlight the person, directly or indirectly. Highlight only the issue. Professional differences are appreciated as long as they have not become personal.

Avoid capital letters: Uppercase is treated as yelling and shouting.

You may underline or colour the font in a different shade to bring about an impact to the main points of your mail, especially if it is a long one. But use this feature very cautiously.

Ensure that you run spellcheck before you forward your mail. Grammatical errors and wrong spelling on a regular basis is a reflection of a casual attitude.

Avoid using BCC (blind copy). If you do want to share, you are advised to forward the mail after sending it the first time.

### SMS/MMS

One of the best gifts to mankind is the recent technology innovation – SMS. It has gradually become one of the important ways of communication. It is the best tool to silently convey your greetings, wishes, meeting updates, whereabouts, business updates and even romance. It is not interfering as it gives the receiver the freedom to reply at one's own pace, or to not reply at all. But as we know, every coin has two sides, and so does SMS. SMS keeps you outside meetings even if you are physically present in the meeting. And that may be detrimental to your growth, as in likelihood you would have missed out on the essentials of the meeting. Also, SMS always keeps you busy with your phone and thus has the potential of making or breaking relationships.

Another con that comes to mind with regard to SMS is that it tempts you not to think much before speaking and writing. It is convenient, so you tend to revert or forward sometimes without thinking. All you have to do is write what's on your mind and press that send button. You might have come across some relationships breaking due to SMS. While on the other hand, relationships are maintained through an occasional SMS as well, and does not eat into your time, but gives the receiver the feeling that they are on your mind. Keep certain 'musts' in mind while using SMS. It can go either way.

Do not keep your phone in your hand when in a meeting. In case you tend to look at it again and again, keep it in the phone case, or on the table or in your pocket.

Avoid using SMS language with seniors like spelling 'you' as 'u', 'take' as 'tk', it might create a casual approach towards your seniors, and especially in the Indian context, not many seniors like to be taken casually. Do not forward or write vulgar jokes to your seniors unless it is initiated by him/her at least twice or thrice or more. Most of them do not appreciate it. Apply exactly the same caution and logic as in forwarding non-official mails, which we have covered in detail a little while back.

While forwarding, ensure that you delete the name of the sender. In case you are keen to share daily thoughts with your colleagues, do so with people you consider your friends at work, not with people you are not friendly with. Also keep in mind the timing of the SMS. Early-morning and late-evening SMSes are not appreciated from unknown people, only from people you are personally close to.

### Chat

Although 'Chat' has not been taken much advantage of or is not in fashion yet in the professional world, it is growing as fast as the SMS revolution, among young and tech-savvy professionals. It is faster, online, private, and non-intrusive. Chat is used more often in your personal relationships and for having fun with your friends. However this mode is slowly and marginally taking on a sizeable ratio of corporate daily communication.

Besides keeping in mind all the dos and don'ts that we have already mentioned in emailing and SMSing, some of the important things to keep in mind while chatting is that it is as good as talking to a person, only online. Some of the points to be kept in mind are given below.

Using slang and short words during chat is quite acceptable and is a trend among similar groups and levels. If the same is used with juniors and seniors, it gets awkward.

You do not yell at people while talking to them in person; similarly avoid writing in capital letters.

You do not pronounce words incorrectly, similarly ensure your spellings are accurate. One letter here and there could change the whole meaning of the sentence.

There is something called ASL in chatting. Age, Sex and Location. Avoid asking age and sex at an early stage. These are personal. Asking for location is okay.

While chatting, the use of vulgar words and abuse is easy as it is rather simple to get away from a person. Never take advantage of this situation. Leave the situation or quit an argument if it is not leading to any consensus or agreement. It is anyway not going to either help or enhance chances of your career growth, right?

**Letters and Faxes**

This mode of communication is dying fast, ever since email technology has come into the picture. Letters require more energy and other related formalities to post and send. One has to wait for delivery and even wait for confirmation from the receiver. How to write and what to write could be based on situation and subject. Let us find a common ground of what general situations may comprise of, and that is what we will focus on.

Any letter should not be written without keeping the receiver or audience in mind. If you know your audience well then you will know what they would understand and what information they would require. Keep your receiver and audience in mind. Your initials, words and abbreviation of the body and the conclusion of the letter will change accordingly. You cannot use technical jargon or slangs or abbreviations. Even if you are writing a complaint, ensure that you are polite and courteous. You can always convey harsh messages with friendly words.

**Handwriting/Signature**

It is said and believed that the handwriting of a person depicts his/her characteristics. Straight and clear writing is appealing. If you know your handwriting is not legible, ensure you write slowly and clearly.

One's signature is a matter of pride for everyone. We would think your signature is your style statement, so spend some time on finding yourself a great looking signature! Ensure your signature does not take more space than is specified. Generally, there is a business format with space for signature that is defined. Your signature should be within that space and you must ensure that you are not over-signing and crossing other's space or hogging extra space. Should you do that, you will be perceived as being a bully and being aggressive without a cause.

All signature sequence should be in ascending order, if the signature has to take place between three or more levels. Junior most should sign on the extreme left, then middle and the senior most on the extreme right side of the paper or cheque. If more than two levels have to sign on one paper, it is better to write in rows. Junior most in the top row and so on.

Whew! Wasn't that quite a bit? I think it is time to take a break! In fact, it was worth spending time on such an important aspect of building your impression and career. Trust us – written communication (especially emails) takes up almost 30 per cent to 40 per cent of your daily routine and hence it is important for you to sharpen your writing skills. And, with this, you have also covered almost 30 per cent of your book. We just said 'your book'; yes it is yours because it's been written for you, it belongs to you.

These sessions are not about bed-time reading. The sessions have to be understood by you thoroughly so that the same can be implemented by you to further your career growth. Please try and grasp as much as you can; try and implement what you have read the previous day into your day-to-day life at office. It is unlike fiction where if you do not even understand or miss a couple of pages, you will still be able to catch up rather well in the later pages. So, it is suggested that you read this book with breaks and read it with a fresh mind.

Let's take a tea break here and catch up after a refreshing mug of tea ... Sanjiv takes one-and-a-half spoons of sugar with milk ... Mamata drinks black tea, no sugar.

Should we get on to our new topic, which is yet another interesting and very important topic?

## SPOKEN

So far we have dealt with written communication, which is poles apart from oral communication. You will see how, in the pages to come.

**Body Language:** Did you ever realise that unspoken words could mean much more than spoken words? There's this popular song, that goes – 'It's only words ... words are all I have to take your heart away'. It may work to take hearts away. Yes it may. But it will not take you on to the accelerated career growth path all of you are looking for. And, a small word of advice, your high accelerated career growth would more or less ensure the 'heart taking' part of it, so for starters we shall concentrate on ways to get ahead in our professional lives. Anyway jokes apart, let's get serious and get to one of the most important aspects of spoken communication, i.e. BODY LANGUAGE.

This is a very vast subject. So vast that many books have been and can be written addressing only this subject. As we had mentioned in the beginning of the book, it's vast enough to complicate it to the extent that you will struggle to remember every 'good' gesture and 'bad' gesture and appear like a mess. Our take on this is, if you mean well, you will portray well. Your intention drives what you say, how you say it and what you do. Keep your intentions clear.

However, here we will try to give you some basics that you must keep in mind.

**Maintain eye contact** – Look straight in the eyes of the person you are talking to. DO NOT keep shifting your eyes left and right. If the stare gets a little too much, just look away for a bit, and get right back into looking straight in the eyes.

**Sit straight and smart** – Sitting posture while talking is of utmost importance. Try not to bend your shoulders while sitting. Drooping shoulders do not spell style nor energy.

**Bend forward a bit** – This shows you are a keen listener. It also shows that you are indeed interested in striking a conversation, and that it has value to you to have this conversation. It makes the other person feel important, and you already know everybody wants to feel important.

**Do not slouch** – This is an absolute 'don't'. This directly portrays indifference and a rather casual approach. Worse still, it might portray a 'know it all' attitude.

**Do not stray off your seat** – Make sure you are comfortably seated on the chair and are not at the edge.

**Hands** – Don't play with your ring or chain or a bracelet. Focus your complete attention on the individual in front of you. Don't throw around your hands too much, neither keep them clasped. And definitely do not talk with your hands folded. This is by far the most defensive body language, that needn't be used with a colleague. Pointing fingers and talking is not acceptable at all.

**Legs** – Crossed legs look very elegant and confident. If you are not in the habit of crossing your legs then just keep them parallel together. Do not squeeze them into each other, neither open them wide apart.

**Smile** – Last but not the least is this most beautiful gesture called the 'SMILE'. It breaks all barriers, nullifies negativity, and brings a sense of warmth to all involved in the conversation. This is one gesture that can make or break your conversation. It's 'oh so' important.

So much about body language. This should be enough to get you going. Let's get on to the other important aspects of spoken communication.

When you are in the middle of a heated discussion, give a pause and then react – you need not react immediately. It seems to the other person that you are in control, calm and composed, and you are also taken more seriously. You definitely want to counter allegations made against you. And you should, but, do it in a way that you are accepted. Give the other person a chance to talk it out, whatever is on his/her mind. In the meanwhile collect your thoughts, pause for a while, then start your counterreactions.

### Golden rule

Take any conversation as a discussion rather than an argument. An argument will never take you to any conclusion, whereas a mature discussion will.

If you are unsure, always say 'I will get back to you' instead of blabbering something that doesn't make sense.

## Speak with Confidence

Always speak confidently, never mind how confident you actually are regarding what you are talking about. The other person should not be able to sense your nervousness. It's a human tendency to take advantage of weaker prey. So, again our advice to you is to say 'I will get back to you' if you are unsure.

If you have nothing worthwhile to say, PLEASE KEEP QUIET; do not speak out and prove beyond doubt that you indeed had nothing worthwhile to say. There's this proverb, that all of us have grown up with, which is 'Silence is golden'. Believe us, it helps – specially when you are unsure or not knowledgeable enough on the topic.

Think in the language that you are going to speak in. For example, if you are going to put your views across in English, then think in English. Very often, we find ourselves thinking in our mother tongue and translating and speaking it out in English. Avoid doing this.

When you want to speak one-on-one with your senior, or for that matter with anyone, it works better to rehearse what you wish to discuss. There may be many deal-clinching points you would otherwise miss. Even before making a presentation, always present your PPT to yourself first. You'll see the difference!

Have you ever noticed if you are interrupted most of the time when you are making your point or if you are able to capture the attention of the people around when you are speaking? Whether there is a pin-drop silence in the room when you are speaking or if there are murmurs? Does the presenter or chairperson have to request all to be silent if you are speaking? If yes, you need tips on public speaking. That encompasses everything from your voice, tone, pitch, modulation, choice of words and sentences.

**Golden rule**

Speak a little higher than your normal pitch.
You will be noticed.

To further develop your confidence while speaking, ensure that

- You know the topic/subject/point you want to speak on inside out.
- You have some information/views to share.
- If you have neither of the above, please do not speak.

Even if you excel in voice, modulation, etc., you lose your charm if you are unable to add value to any topic. The audience will be utterly disinterested as soon as they see you as a speaker. When we say speaker, we don't mean you addressing a large gathering like a politician; we mean even speaking at meetings in the office, or addressing your own team for that matter.

### Accent

Mind your pronunciation but never mind your accent. If you speak English with a tinge of your native accent, it doesn't matter. As long as you speak grammatically correct English and as long as you are able to get your thoughts across to the other person, it's all right. In fact, if you try to put on an accent, it sounds out of place and sometimes hilarious. Of course, there are times in this global business atmosphere, where you might be required to put on the accent of the person you are speaking to, but for that you will be given ample training and it will be easy enough for you to adopt. But, under normal business circumstances, please speak confidently and do not worry over your accent.

### Greetings

You start your day with greetings. Make it a point to do so and take the opportunity to use names while greeting people in the morning. Greetings are essential, names are important.

To have your own style of wishing people good morning is a good idea. Raising your hand to your chest, showing the victory sign, or saluting with your hand is a reflection of a happy mood. For a more personal greeting, winking to close friends (of course while being cautions of this form of salutation while greeting someone from the opposite gender) could also be your fashion statement. Yes style quotient helps even in the corporate world. Just be cautious that you don't overdo it otherwise you will not be taken seriously. It must be confusing when we say 'do this but don't overdo it' for every small gesture, but the key to success lies in balancing. You are expected to do a balancing act ALL THE TIME, on all occasions. The better you are at balancing, the easier it is for you!

If you run into a person several times a day, a big smile is not necessary. But do maintain eye contact and maybe bend your head forward just slightly so that the person does not feel ignored. Never ignore a person.

Avoid going to the boss's cabin to wish them, as a habit. You will be seen as a pest and a pot full of butter. You know what we mean!

If you sit inside a cabin and someone is at your door, how do you react? Now this is a tad bit more complicated. We would like to touch upon it though, as it is important. If it is your team member, you may continue to sit, but look up, smile and gesture for him/her to come in. If it is a peer you are very friendly with, you may go ahead with the same treatment. However, if it is a peer you are formal with, you need not really get up from your seat, but do bend your torso forward as an indication that s/he is welcome. If it is your senior, without a question (whether you are friendly or not), stand up and shake hands with them if you are meeting for the first time during the day, otherwise just stand around and wait for your instructions. Wave your right hand towards the chair in front of your desk, inviting him/her to sit.

Of course the main ingredient is a SMILE. Don't forget to smile. At everyone!

## Handshake

Another controversial topic. Especially in India. This is really tricky. With a lady it is best not to take the first step towards a handshake. Wait for her to extend her hand, if at all. Otherwise just ape what she does, like saying namaste or nodding. Do not shake hands when your hands are wet. Due to rising infectious diseases, if you are suffering from an infection, you are expected to avoid shaking hands. You can avoid this by not raising your hand and politely informing them by saying, 'Sorry, you would like to avoid shaking my hand as I have been suffering from a bout of cold and cough' for example. A handshake can tell a lot about your personality and confidence level. There are many details written about what makes a perfect handshake. However, we think in the practical world, a firm shake while maintaining eye-contact and wearing a smile is all that is required. By 'firm' we don't mean crushing the other person's fingers. Just be firm enough. The worst you can do is to give a limp handshake or a quick one, as if you are in a hurry to go. When you are shaking hands with someone, be present there completely – physically of course you have to be, but even mentally. Be attentive. And do remember to leave a comfort space of about a three foot distance from the other person.

## Introduction

Your name – preferably your first name with a pause followed by your surname; this should be followed by your function and the role you are handling.

There is a protocol to be followed during introduction. The more senior person should be the one who everybody else is introduced to. For e.g. – 'Mr General Manager, may I introduce Mr Team Leader'. A tricky situation is when a Team Leader, who is your company's client, has come to meet your General Manager, for example. Here the thing to remember is, the client is more important than even your highest boss. So the client takes the position of the higher authority.

Unlike social situations where a lady is introduced first, or an older peron is given the position of authority, it is not so in the corporate world. In all professional situations, designation and position is to be considered, irrespective of gender or age. This is to be followed through without exception. When you are being introduced to someone always stand up and shake hands. If you are unable to stand, make a gesture like sticking your neck out, nodding and leaning forward slightly, to show that you are accepting the introduction wholeheartedly.

While introducing someone, never make the mistake of pronouncing a person's name incorrectly. This creates the most disastrous impression. In India especially, we have such diverse regions with diverse names, and it may sometimes be impossible for you to read a name and pronounce it. If you are in doubt, always make sure you ask, rather than pronouncing a name wrong. A name is a very initimate part of a person's life and usually people are unwilling to accept your error when it comes to their name. Even a name wrongly spelt can get a person furious. Be very particular when it comes to names. If you have forgotten someone's name, apologise and ask. There's no harm in that. In fact, try and remember names as much as you can. When you call somebody by his/her name, there is an instant connection as everybody likes to be remembered. Read up on how to remember names and practise it. It will take you a long way. NAME is a sensitive topic, to be kept in mind at all times.

You may call people by their first name or second name or 'Sir' and 'Madam', as in the culture of the organisation you work for. Nowadays in certain organisations, a junior executive also calls the chairman of the company by first name. It depends on the culture adopted by your company. However, if you happen to notice that there is no particular culture being followed, you might adopt this. Use 'Ms' or 'Mr' with the second name, if you are meeting a senior/older person for the first time. And continue to use it unless told not to. 'Sir' and 'Madam' are rather outdated now, but then there are some seniors from the old school who still prefer it. So figure out for yourself what works with whom. Be aware and adopt the right way.

Another thing here is the presentation of business cards. This seemingly mundane activity happens to be a highly impacting one. The process you follow while distributing your business cards says so much about you as a professional, you would not even imagine. However, like all other things, it is not rocket science (unless you want to make it into one).

Keep your business cards in a place that is easily accessible so that you do not have to fumble while looking for it. Place them in a card holder or something similar, which will save the cards from being crumpled, dirty or soiled by your sweat.

While presenting your business card, take pride in your card (it shows in your body language), look into the eyes of the person you are presenting it to, and hand the card with both your hands. Make sure the card faces up and all the letters are facing the person receiving your card. Don't forget your smile. That should become your very nature. A soft smile at all times.

Similarly, while accepting a card, follow exactly the same process. Look in the other person's eyes, and accept it with both hands. Even if the card given to you is of no value to you, treat it with respect because it means a lot to the other person. Read the card briefly as if you are really interested, even if you are not, and tuck it in a respectable place. Do not put it in your back pocket. The best place is the front pocket for men and the purse for women.

Even if you have already presented your card, do not ask for a senior person's card. Wait for the senior to give it to you.

Always introduce your juniors as your colleagues; never mention that they are part of your team or report to you. Other people will figure out your position and your power during the course of the meeting. If you give respect to your juniors, they will respect you too.

Introduce yourself on the phone if your recipient does not know you. The sequence goes like this – your company name first, followed by your name and the purpose of the call.

While receiving a call, always mention your first name rather than saying hello. With mobile technology, we call people not places. Although your caller might know you, it is always better to give your name so that they immediately connect to who they've called.

If your colleague's cellphone rings in front of you, you should never make an attempt to pick the call. Just in case you are in a situation where you have to pick up somebody's phone in his/her absence, ensure you reveal your identity immediately. And then add that the number called is correct, however the person is not available. Always leave it to the caller for choice whether s/he would like to leave any message for him/her. Anything spoken beyond this would seem like interfering in somebody else's private space, and that is the worst you could do – it is almost as bad as peeping into someone else's computer screen, or opening an envelope that is marked to another person. All said and done, however close you are to a person, NO ONE appreciates a nosy and intrusive person. On the other hand, everybody appreciates a person who is non-interfering and not peeking into his/her life, personal or professional. However, if the office extension of your colleague is ringing, do pick it up without fail, and follow the same rules of identifying yourself, taking a message if the caller wants to leave one, etc.

### Compliments

These occasions are great opportunities for you for bonding and to express friendliness. Complimenting people definitely requires confidence and tact. It is an art. Some people have a natural flair for complimenting others. It comes naturally to them. However this only comes with experience and gaining expertise over the years for the rest of us.

A compliment can sometimes sound outright false. If you don't mean it, don't say it. Do not use compliments as a tool to please your boss or colleagues, or to make up after an argument. Compliment someone only if you really mean it. Otherwise people can see through it, and that is one of the worst images you could build for yourself.

### Wishes

Always make it a point to call and wish close colleagues. SMS is a very easy way to reach out and express your affection. But if time and situation permits, do call and wish your colleagues personally. It does make a difference. If you are hard-pressed for time, at least try and mention the name of the recipient in the SMS as this personalises the SMS to a great extent.

Wish the person while making eye-to-eye contact and with a handshake. Hold the person's hand for at least three to five seconds and with the other hand, hold the elbow of the person you are wishing. This posture expresses affection and sincerity while wishing someone and is quite acceptable with both genders. Do mention that you will pray for their happiness and good health. 'God bless' adds that extra zing and value to your greetings.

Maintain a diary or record of friends and colleagues whom you would like to keep in touch with and wish on such occasions. It helps in creating a better impression over the years, if you remember to call and wish people. Remember, what you give in life, you always get back in a certain way.

This is a great tool to keep your old relationships with your ex-colleagues and ex-bosses. It pays in the long run and it is one of the signs of being a good human being.

**Conference Call/Video Conferencing**

To save time and cost, conference calls and video conferences are catching up fast across organisations and nations. With mobile technology, it has further become friendly and easy for call conferencing between two or more people. You need to ensure certain manners during CC and VC; else it could be irritating for the others.

Always take permission from callers and parties before joining them. After joining the call, introduce each other if the parties are not known to each other already; if they are known parties, do inform both sides by identifying the members. Keeping it a secret and not mentioning who is a part of the call may have adverse effects. It may result in losing the trust of either party.

Ensure you know the CC equipment well – How to be on speaker mode, how to put a call on hold, etc. Putting the phone on mute when you are not speaking is a must. After the introductions are through, immediately go on mute. Ensure you choose a quiet place in advance. A slight disturbance in the background can be caught by a sensitive mike. Avoid joining calls while driving or when out on the field.

Take the lead to introduce your team as well if you are all from the same location, to save time.

If you want to ask questions, make it a point to mention your name before you ask your question, everytime. It helps other attendees to recognise and relate to you.

After you finish your point, say 'over' and go to mute mode again. Similar rules apply for VC as well.

While on VC, ensure that you are well-covered by the camera and always be attentive with body posture. Here again, keeping in mind the session on body language would help.

If you take a CC on your mobile, ensure that you do not take any other call until you're done with the CC. By taking another call you will put CC on hold, and the rest of the attendees will not be able to continue with the CC until you finish. There was a situation when one of our colleagues took a call on his mobile, and the CC instrument was not on mute, and we overheard the entire conversation that he had with his fiancée. Just after he ended his call, my boss asked him a question on his data, and he was completely lost. He kept fumbling and blabbered some nonsensical information and we all laughed out loud! Such could be the repercussions of not following these simple rules.

While on the topic of phones and calls, let us also mention a few telephone manners that you may adopt even while talking to a single individual and not necessarily a conference. When you are on a call, don't let anything distract you. Reading a mail or writing a note is not advisable as the person on the other side may notice your indifference to the call. Eating and drinking while on call is an absolute no-no. Be attentive and talk to the point when on a business call. It's best to jot down the points before making the call so that you don't miss out on any topic and have to call later for the same thing. As much as possible try and avoid calling people after business hours or on holidays and weekends, unless it is absolutely urgent. And if you do, be sure to apologise first before taking your conversation any further. If you happen to take a call for your colleague, and the caller wishes to leave a message, please take it down sincerely, and convey it to your colleague as soon as you can. In case you have dialled a wrong number, say sorry. Don't just hang up. Last but not the least, DO NOT ever leave a ringing office extension unattended. Even if it means walking a few steps to pick the call. If it's a regular occurrence with some colleagues, have a chat with that colleague and urge them to either put their extension on silent or better still, to divert to voice mail.

In case of a cellphone though, there are a few other things to keep in mind. Keeping jazzy songs as your ringtone and that too on loud mode is not appreciated. It's most preferred to use formal ringtones while at work. But if you must keep a song, make sure it is on the lowest volume possible. There are times that your service provider fails to provide you with adequate network, in which case, do not shout and scream over the phone. Remember that the person on the other end cannot hear you because of the network, not because of your volume. Keep your mouth close to the phone and you may also cover your mouth, guiding your voice towards the microphone. That way your voice will be audible even if you speak very softly. Always ask the person if it is a good time to talk, before starting your conversation.

To be able to follow all that is covered in this session will require time and concentration from you. A lot of these attributes are developed over a period of time, and with experience – like sharpening your pronunciation, grammar and English as a language. But most of this can be developed by keeping note of all activities on a day-to-day basis. Note your behaviour in relation to what we have said and make mental notes. That way you will be able to imbibe all these lessons. This is as important (if not more) as your technical subjects.

Your personality is a mix of your words and appearance. Once you have introduced yourself and spoken, all eyes are on you, to watch how you present yourself.

Even if your communication has become an art, your appearance and how you carry yourself, might take you for a toss. But at the same time if your appearance is perfect as per time and occasion, it adds bonus points to your impression. So how you can make your appearance a part of your attitude, and turn heads wherever you go, is what the next session is all about.

"Two **A**s that go along with you wherever you go. "Attitude and Appearance"."

# Session II

# APPEARANCE

You might have read books and heard statements/quotes like 'You are what you wear', 'You are what you eat', 'You are what you talk', etc. That means that everything you do describes your character, and your preferences, and in a way it reflects in the way you eat and talk, and the clothes you wear. Similarly, your choice of fashion, colour, and style defines your appearance and your attitude. And it also creates a strong opinion about you. You might be underdressing or overdressing or dressing appropriately, but the point is that you should be carrying yourself well. If anyone were to make a comment about your appearance, you can reflect on what you would like them to say or what you would like to hear about yourself. Carry yourself well. In this session we will focus on how to carry yourself and improve your appearance. In fact, the main focus of this book is to describe how you carry yourself through any situation or occasion in the corporate world. In this session we wish to give you a basic idea on how to carry yourself with your look.

What is actually meant by carrying your look well? It basically means that your look should soothe the eyes and hearts of people around you in contrast to being an 'eyesore', as they say. Do people enjoy looking at you? Do they feel good to talk to you? Do you sound good to them? Furthermore, do they get distracted while talking, listening or looking at you?

The adverse effect of not being appropriately dressed is that you will never know what you are losing every day, or about the many opportunities that might have come your way. The corporate world is all about references; people do carry good and passionate people along. All opportunities can never be known to you, but it can be known to someone whom you have known, and that person remembers you as someone who is well-groomed and that you carry yourself well.

It would be rather easy for us to outline for you what to wear, and list down dresses, colours, and styles, but that is not the purpose of this lesson. You ought to be interested in contemporary fashion and colours and patterns so you keep yourself abreast of the current trends and style. We wish to focus on some of the basics and some practical aspects of how to carry yourself, but keeping with the times, you have to take it on yourself.

But before we go on to dressing, hairstyle, and accessories, the important aspects to grooming are mentioned below:

- Keep yourself clean and fresh.
- Care for your hands and feet like you care for your face and hair. It is as important if not more. Keep your fingers and toes clean, with your nails cut and neat.
- Moisturise your arms, legs, palms and feet right after your bath.

- Take immediate precautions for body odour and bad breath.

Further into this session we wish to deal with women and men in separate sections for obvious reasons. As usual, ladies first.

**Women**

When it comes to women, choices for dresses and accessories are plenty. But what is more important are the stares of men; which is a day-to-day scenario that every woman has to go through and handle with tact. Every woman would know about the flaws and the highlights of her body. Hiding your flaws and highlighting the better aspects is a smart way to present yourself. For example, if you have wide hips but shapely shoulders, tops that hide your hips and highlight the shape of your shoulders will work well for you. There are volumes written on this subject, we do not wish to dwell on that at the moment. However, we wish to draw your attention to the fact that these are highly important aspects and hence must not be ignored but must be given due diligence by you. Do read up on the best clothing styles (Indian and Western) for your body type and select your clothes accordingly. You will spend the same amount of money, yet look better. There is a lot written on which colour would suit you best depending on your anatomy and skin colour. Another important aspect is to dress according to your age. Blindly following fashion that may not go well with your age is hazardous. However, all in all, the single most important aspect is appropriate dressing. Different occasions call for different kinds of dressing. Let us cover this a little more in detail. For day-to-day work, you may choose to wear a simple salwaar suit, as that seems to be the most preferred among working Indian women today. Or, you may choose a simple shirt with a pair of smart trousers (again choose your trouser style depending on your anatomy). For regular reviews and meetings this itself should suffice. However, should you have a meeting with seniors visiting from the corporate office or clients, make it a point to wear something more formal, like a formal western suit or a saree or a churidaar suit, preferably with collars and well tailored/fitted. On Fridays you may try out your casuals, short kurtis teamed with well-fitted denims (not torn denims that are in fashion every now and then) and flat chappals and dangling earrings, etc. But by all means, avoid wearing tight T-shirts and those that have slogans and artwork that attract unnecessary attention.

Another important aspect is how much skin you can expose. The safest bet here is to not expose any skin at all while in an office environment – no cleavage, no low-waist pants, no belly button. No doubt there are women who look extremely attractive when they know just how much to expose and know how to do it elegantly. However, in an office 'nil' is the best choice. There is a fear of not being taken seriously, or distracting colleagues from the point you are trying to make as a professional. There are some things in this world over which we do not have control, and must accept the reality as it stands. That is wise dressing.

How you walk is something you must keep in mind too. Wearing a great shirt and looking good in itself would not be of much help. We have noticed some colleagues who wear a smart suit and walk like they are wearing denims. Or wearing a saree and stomping up and down the office. It's very important to walk with confidence and at the same time to be graceful. You should not stomp up and down, nor should you be too demure. Maintain a balance.

Every woman would know whether she looks good in Indian outfits or Western outfits. If you are not sure, ask your family members and very close friends or close office colleagues of both sexes. You will gain confidence and avoid unnecessary comments on your dresses.

Keep it simple, but fashionable. It is definitely possible. Let's look at suits/Indian outfits.

## Suits/Sarees

Whether it is a tight churidaar suit or salwar suit, suits are the most common daily wear for professional working women in India.

Ensure that your suits are of the latest fashion. There are certain colours and motifs that are in fashion from time to time. You must keep an eye out for that. We don't mean for you to be a fashion victim and change your entire wardrobe as and when the fashion changes. All we ask is if you can alter your long kurtas into short ones, if short kurtas are in fashion. Even having just a few items from the latest fashion would help you juggle with the old and new, so that you don't look out of place. You would also have noticed that the old styles come back into fashion in a year or two, in which case, you may do well by storing your old suits and getting them out when they are back in fashion.

Long or deep cuts in the neck and back of the suit is not recommended. Usually the most recommended neckline is a simple round neck with a small slit, or something with collars. While sitting down or bending over, your skin should not be visible from the sides or back. Also, we lay maximum importance to the fit of your dress. Clothes that are too tight according to your physique or too loose do not reflect well. Both look sloppy. We in India are so fortunate to be able to get clothes tailored to our size without spending a fortune for it, unlike in the Western countries. Let's make good use of this facility. You must ensure that you identify one good and permanent tailor for your clothes, one that understands your taste and your physique as well. Ready-made suits are also available in plenty these days and are quite fashionable and very reasonable too. But the hitch is, as soon as you walk out of the store after your purchase you may find two others already wearing the exact same dress. Here also you could style your clothes by mixing and matching the bottom and the dupatta to create your own unique style. You can retain your individuality and at the same time get yourself a fashionable outfit. There are a lot of large stores today that offer you this option.

Make the best use of your dupatta and do keep good control over it. A great dupatta teamed with even a simple suit can make a huge impact. Also, teaming different dupattas with different suits gives you variety without having to actually invest in a new suit.

Sleeves should ideally be kept at half, quarter or full. If you do have to wear sleeveless kurtas due to very warm weather, or because you simply enjoy wearing it that way, make sure sleeves are well-fitted to your armpit and take extra care of your underarms. A loose arm hole in a sleeveless outfit will jeopardise your efforts to 'not expose'. And to an onlooker, there is nothing more disgusting than the sight of badly maintained underarms.

Be careful while choosing the fabric and the colour. Make sure it is not too thin that it shows your undergarments. It's advisable to wear a slip if you are even slightly in doubt. Always remember you are in an office environment, so your image should be well-protected. You can always try out your other fashion ideas while you are out with your friends and family.

The saree is a blessing to an Indian woman. There is no outfit that accentuates the physique of an Indian woman better than a saree. Also it is the most elegant piece of clothing. It is best suited to any occasion and every Indian woman, no matter what her physique is like, looks absolutely gorgeous in a saree. There is a wide variety to choose from. All fabrics work well in an office environment except very thin ones that are see-through. Avoid wearing heavily woven silk sarees, or heavily embroidered ones. Save those for special occasions. Sarees that you wear to office (even if you are scheduled for a big meeting) should be utterly simple, and the motifs and the colours should not be too loud. Wearing a very gaudy or heavy saree even if you are a newlywed is not recommended.

The aspect while wearing a saree that deserves the maximum attention is the blouse. Unlike salwaar suits, your blouse can have a slightly deeper neck behind, but not in front. Exposing even half-an-inch of cleavage is shabby. The best sleeve length is up to your elbow, but if you are very uncomfortable with that length you may have it a bit shorter. Even sleeveless blouses that are well-fitted look very elegant with a saree. Draping your saree is another aspect. It's best to learn to drape a saree from that gorgeous aunt who you have admired since your childhood. How you look in a saree is highly dependent on the way you drape it. The length is something you must keep an eye out for. Don't wear the saree first and then your high heels. The length will go haywire. Drape your saree while you are wearing the exact sandals that you will wear with it. Make sure your navel is well covered with the pallu and that your pallu is well pinned at your shoulder. Use pins whenever you feel uncomfortable. While using pins, use a small piece of paper so that the saree doesn't tear. These small tips will anyway be given to you by your mother/aunt whose borrowed saree will most probably be the first saree that you will wear.

The flip side of the saree story is the time taken to drape it. Also, you have to be very confident walking in it. Walking in a saree needs practise and you will never gain enough confidence if you don't practise. So, we would advise you to take the pains to get used to wearing a saree, because it is a boon to an Indian woman. You will feel very confident and look gorgeous wearing a saree. It is worth the effort.

While wearing a saree if you have to bend for some reason, sit straight down without bending your back forward. Fold your knees, sit and get up straight.

**Trousers/Shirts**

This is quite well-accepted in any part of the country over the last two decades. It is also very comfortable and gives you the freedom to run about getting your jobs done. It's among the most formal and yet comfortable work clothes. All a working woman probably needs is about eight to ten smart shirts; a black pair of trousers, a beige one and maybe a white one.

That's it. That could well be your wardrobe for dressing from Monday to Thursday.

Generally in India, ladies prefer sharp and primary colours, but that generally does not gel well with the corporate world. Ensure all your Western suits are of gentle and muted colours, black, shades of grey, shades of brown and blue. Shirts should again fit you well and be made with collars. With suits, light shirts go well, patterns of stripes and checks are also fashionable.

Trousers should only be loose from the bottom and should fit you well at your hips and thighs. Generally, it should be parallel and fall straight. However, if you are getting it tailored, you may discuss this aspect with your tailor.

Do keep an eye on the fashion aspect. Your suits should not be too old-fashioned.

### Footwear

You must avoid wearing flat sandals at your workplace, unless you have been advised by a doctor not to wear heels. Even then we would urge you to consult your doctor, if you could manage a small heel, say one inch. On the other hand, heels at the most should be two or two-and-a-half inches; beyond that it will restrict your walk. It is said that your brain works at the speed of your walk. Ensure your heels allow swift and comfortable walking.

A rubber sole is preferable as it does not make noise on any kind of floor. Making noise while walking may be an irritant to your colleagues. You must be careful not to disturb your colleagues, who might be immersed in work.

Keeping your feet firm on the floor while walking helps you not make a dragging sound while walking. It is said, the more you drag your feet while walking, the more you kill your conscience.

Loose shoes will hamper your walk and will not allow you to keep your feet firm on the floor. Make sure your shoes fit you well.

Dust on shoes reflects how much dirt is in your heart. Clean shoes are recommended. Pure leather or good quality non-leather is recommended. Closed or open shoes, both are acceptable. Torn or broken shoes are a reflection of unorganised character.

Never compromise on your footwear, do invest time and money to buy good shoes. Basically, one which fits well. World-renowned companies spend millions in research to make scientifically and technically good shoes. This is an investment and not a buy. You are investing money in your health in a way, when you are buying the right shoes.

Never wear sports shoes to office, especially the white ones with colourful logos of the shoe company. Save them for 'Annual Sports Day' or a team picnic. Never wear them to office, even if it is a casual dressing day. We notice a number of people wearing sports shoes/sneakers to office. That must be avoided by all means. If you absolutely must wear them, then choose brown or black colours.

### Hairstyle

Hairstyling is an individual's interpretation of him or herself. It is indeed a very integral part of your personality. It's god's grace what kind of hair you have – straight, wavy, curly, etc. Fortunately each type has a fall and enormous style of its own.

Your facial features should not be overshadowed by your hairstyle. If you are not comfortable with your features then you may adopt a style which helps you overshadow your features with a good hairstyle.

Your hair falling on your forehead in front of your eyes looks very untidy and is definitely not a great fashion idea in the corporate world. Make sure that your hair is cut short or tied well.

Clean and dandruff-free hair is necessary. Regular wash or shampoo followed by conditioner for silky and shiny hair is recommended. The shoulder of your suit or shirt covered with dandruff is totally unacceptable.

Comb your hair regularly, it helps you keep it clean and also maintain the fall. Do carry your brush/comb in your purse and comb your hair, twice or thrice or whenever you have been out and have come back to office again.

Unique artificial hair colour does not go well in most of the industry unless your role demands it. Of course, muted and almost natural colours like brown are quite acceptable, but not red for example, or very light colours. While dyeing your hair, pay attention that it doesn't look patchy.

And yes, make sure your hair doesn't appear oily, be it long or short!

**Make-up**

Make-up really depends on the industry that you work in. Hospitality and entertainment industry employees have to take extra care. However, slight make-up is an absolute must irrespective of the industry. Basic make-up would mean kohl application, or eyeliner on your eyelids and lipstick. This is the bare minimum. While applying lipstick make sure it doesn't spread outside your lips. That looks very clumsy. You may use a lip liner and then fill in your lips with your preferred colour. Slightly more elaborate make-up would include some eye shadow, mascara and blush. Ensure your make-up is subtle and light and you cannot go wrong.

If you wear a bindi, it should be a plain and small one. Designer bindis and complicated ones are best kept for special occasions.

**Other Little Things that Make an Impression**

Cleanliness and hygiene is not to be compromised at any cost. You may compromise on anything else if you must, but not on cleanliness. This is the most attractive aspect of a person's personality.

Keep both your finger nails and toenails clean and cut regularly. We have seen even senior people ignoring this. It leaves a very ugly impression if you do that. If you prefer to wear your nails long, ensure they are shaped well. Pedicure and manicure is recommended at least once a month in summer and twice a month in winter. You need not have to spend a lot of money at beauty parlours. Get it done in a parlour once, and see how they do it. Then buy yourself the tools they use, which are found in every cosmetic shop these days, and do it yourself. It gives you confidence to display your hand and fingers to point at screens or at papers. It looks very appealing too, to the onlooker. Wear light-coloured nail polish if you wish to paint your nails.

Waxing of arms, legs and underarms are an absolute must. Here again if you find the beauty salons too expensive, do it by yourself at home. Threading of eyebrows is something you may not attempt to do by yourself, but it is the most inexpensive treatment and gets done in minutes. Bleaching and facials are add-ons and undoubtedly add to hygiene and to a better look.

Ensure your panty line is not showing through especially in today's Western outfits and light-weight trousers. Generally, V-shaped panties stick out and definitely invite people around to stare at you. Wear knicker-shaped panties with trousers and skirts, should you want to avoid those unnecessary glances that will distract people from listening to a brilliant proposition you might be putting forth for their perusal. Also, when you sit while wearing trousers, take utmost care that your panty does not peep out of the waist of your trousers, and also ensure your back is not on display.

Take good care of your bra straps. Straps sticking out in an office environment look very shabby. We understand that it's not always possible to keep a check on it, and sometimes it might accidentally stick out. In which case, the best option is to have an unwritten rule among all female employees in the office to let each other know through a silent gesture, whenever that happens. The same applies when your cleavage peeps out sometimes.

Tattoos should be made on hidden parts of your body. Hands, forearms, neck, etc., are visible in day-to-day working. These style statements are indeed a reflection of your individuality, but they can be flaunted when you are out of office, while hanging out with friends. In an office environment tattoos give a frivolous impression of you, and even if you are otherwise brilliant at your work, there are chances of the same being discounted. It's better to stay conventional in office and earn all that extra money to do your own thing when you are out of office.

Being healthy and fit is also a mantra for success. If you remain sick and unfit often you will surely be left behind. Take care of what you eat and exercise regularly. Not only will you remain healthy from the inside, but you will look good with a better body shape as well. A good body shape adds value to your clothing and personality.

Develop a habit of regular exercise like gymming, yoga, any sport or just plain jogging and walking. It not only keeps your body fit and agile, but also keeps your mind fresh; and keeps you active and less vulnerable to sickness and allergies. This will also keep your skin glowing.

**Men**

It is generally quoted in the work place to 'Dress up for the next level'. If you are able to cope to these standards/rules for yourself, it will definitely give you an edge over the other men around you. A man's dressing sense could be judged by answering a few of the questions listed here.

- Are you looking too casual for your workplace?
- Is your outfit in accordance with your business environment?

- Do you have a sense of combining the right colours?
- Do you have a sense of style of contemporary fashion/patterns; do you manage your look as per the company's image?

Ask yourselves these questions, when you are in front of the mirror checking out your outfit for the day.

The colour and pattern of your outfit is one of the most important parameters for judging a good dressing style and a bad one. Managing a man's wardrobe in today's world is thought of as expensive. As Shakespeare had said, 'Costly thy habit as thy purse can buy.' But let us tell you, you really do not have to be rich to maintain a good wardrobe. There are umpteen 'discount sales' during festival seasons. Pick up your clothes for the year at that time. You do get your incentives once a year. Use that money to dress well and earn more incentives in the bargain. You do not have to dress like fashion models. Neat, clean, sober, refined and contemporary is good enough. In any case corporate colours are limited. Have one of each colour. Or, you may have your own style of wearing only one colour everyday. But, not the same shirt. Well-ironed clothes, which are neat and clean, define the way you carry yourself.

## Suits/Blazers

Suits separate the men from the boys. With a suit you have to adapt your style, class, and look. When you are a junior in the office, you are not really expected to wear a suit, at least in the Indian environment, unless you are in a job that requires you to meet clients. So, when you buy your first suit, make sure you buy a really good quality one, preferably black in colour. There is nothing shoddier than a bad quality suit, which is badly fitted and made of unrefined material. So do wait till you can gather enough money to buy a classy suit. Don't be in a hurry.

The colour of the suit is most important. Pick up corporate colours. Black, shades of grey, blue, shades of brown, navy blue are some of the most acceptable colours and they come with elegant patterns of stripes and checks. Some colours just don't go well in suits, like white or light green, etc.

Choose a classic design which is timeless and you can wear it for at least two to three years. Three buttons are the most common fit and are a timeless style. Three-piece suits and double-breasted suits are now completely out of fashion. Do not wear over the top or cutting-edge styles, unless it's a suit for a specific event.

There's nothing to beat a well-fitted suit, which fits your body to your size exactly. Wearing a correctly-fitted suit, to your size, matters a lot while carrying off your suit/blazer. Extra length, extra stretch or strange stretches spoil the look of the suit. Know your exact size and turn around and check your suit from all sides; sit and walk in the suit before you finalise your size. Try the pants and jacket of the suits together to check both fittings. It is recommended to buy ready-made suits as tailor-made suits are rather risky. Any mistake made by the tailor is a sheer waste of time and money. Moreover, ready-made suits of good quality are rather cheap, especially during discount sales.

**Shirt**

Light and plain colour shirts blend best with suits. You may go for bold stripes and checks, but then if your wardrobe is limited, it is best to avoid them. If you have an extensive wardrobe, you may choose from the latest stripes and other patterns. A couple of white shirts are a must for any wardrobe. It looks very formal and goes with everything.

The tip of the collar should be well-pointed and should not be torn or rough. Know the size of your neck as tight or loose collars either make you uncomfortable or spoil the look of a suit and tie. Here again the best fit is very important.

The average life of a shirt is twenty washes, keeping in mind machine wash; if the colour is getting faded or the collar is losing shape, avoid wearing that shirt and replace it with a new one. Please ensure that the cuffs and neck are washed well. Any dirt there looks awful. Also, ensure no sweat stains are visible in the underarms. Sometimes the stains are so tough that they just don't go. Please put in some extra effort there. Neck, cuffs, underarms and buttonhole areas need special attention.

Avoid folding your sleeves while wearing a full sleeve shirt, while at work. Except for Fridays, try and wear full sleeves to office everyday. Tuck your shirt in from all sides well into your belt. Try not to wear thin materials in shirts as they look unprofessional.

### Tie

The colour of the tie should go with or blend with the suit or shirt. Patterns and colours have to be selected with your sense of style. In today's contemporary fashion you will see people carrying sharp and primary colours for ties. The colours which do not gel at all are silver, gold or shiny metallic colours. You can rest assured about most of the other colours. A sense of combining and carrying off a tie with a shirt is an art, which can be learnt. It is a very impacting aspect of your dressing, so try and develop a good sense for it.

Too broad or too thin goes well with neither time nor fashion. Today medium to broad ties are in fashion. We suggest you keep abreast of the latest trends and carry yourself accordingly. Again we are not asking you to be fashion victims, but keeping with the times, more or less, is mandatory.

Double knot and single knot both work well. The knot should not be too tight or too loose. A little fold in a single knot looks trendy.

The length of the tie should reach the buckle of your belt or be an inch-and-a-half below your navel.

**Trousers**

Straight and without pleats are an all-time favourite. It never goes out of fashion. The material should not be too shiny or too rough. Make sure it is well-ironed and has a single crease only. Your trouser should fit you well at the hips. The length should be just right. You will figure this out if you are careful that the front crease does not have more than one fold after it touches your shoe.

**Shoes**

Shoes can make or spoil the entire show. Extreme caution is to be used while choosing your shoes. It is suggested to always take a friend along on a shoe purchase. Shoes that are pointed or flat from the front keep changing as per time and fashion.

Oxford style shoes are timeless and sober and blend with all kinds of suits. If you are planning on having just one or two pairs, it's always better to stick to classic styles. Like a suit, a shoe should be of very good quality.

Wear pure leather rather than artificial leather. The sole of the shoes should have leather in front and rubber in the heel, to ensure there's no sound while walking. At the same time it provides you with comfort on the front part of the foot.

Non-polished shoes are as bad as a man without trousers. Neat and polished shoes are as important as wearing washed clothes each day. It is also said that the more the dirt on your shoes the more the dirt in your heart. Shoes are a true reflection of your grooming. Please do take extra effort to wear the right shoes, and wear it well.

Discard shoes that have lost their shape and have gotten permanent wrinkles or have broken. No extra thread should be seen on shoes. Give preference to laceless shoes unless it is not part of your uniform. Avoid high heels and just go for regular height shoes.

For sports shoes, similar rules apply as mentioned in ladies session.

### Socks

Needless to say, socks should be kept very clean and odour-free. Do not wear socks with holes, especially if there is a religious function in the office and you may be required to take off your shoes. The colour of the socks should match with the colour of your trousers – black socks with black trousers, grey socks with grey trousers is appropriate. Never brown socks with grey trousers or black socks with brown trousers. Avoid wearing white socks with formal shoes.

### Belt and Wallet

The colour of your belt should go with the colour of your shoes. ALWAYS!

The buckle of the belt should be a simple square/rectangle and should be made of metal with either silver or gold shine. Designs of dragons, danger sign and other such emblems can be saved for an evening out with friends.

### Handkerchief

Nowadays, handkerchiefs are sparingly used as tissues seem to have replaced them. However, some men still prefer carrying one, in which case, please remember, this is a total give away of your personal hygiene. Please make sure your handkerchief is sparkling clean and ironed. Yes, ironed. A crumpled handkerchief can look very clumsy. Treat your handkerchief like you treat your shirt. Avoid playing with it or fiddling with it, while you are with somebody. For colour, stick to only white. It may have light stripes at the edges, but no other colour goes for a handkerchief, even if you are a rock star!

### Friday Dressing

Friday dressing is a double-edged sword. Either it can show your sense of style and you carry all outfits well or you take it too casually on Fridays and spoil the reputation you gained over the week. Here are some tips from us that will help you protect your reputation as a good dresser.

Do not wear torn denims even if they are in fashion.

Do not wear shorts and sandals/chappals.

Denim does not go well with sports shoes, which is seen in most parts of India. Wear boots with denim. Sports shoes are meant to be worn for sports, not to office, or even to a party for that matter. Sports shoes can be worn for comfort on a journey, other than that its rightful activity of sport. But, definitely not elsewhere.

Do not wear body-fitting clothes, even if you have a body you can flaunt.

## Hairstyle

Keep your hair fresh by shampooing regularly. Use conditioner and oil to keep that extra shine in your hair. Nowadays you get shampoos in sachets that don't cost much. Use them.

Know what style suits your face. Avoid making high spikes in your hair. Light spikes are acceptable and trendy but keep it sober. Strings of hair sticking behind or falling on your neck are not professional at all. Similarly, a ponytail and long sideburns are not recommended unless it is required for your job. Always keep your hair combed. If you dye your hair, make sure your entire hair sports the same colour. A bad hair dye can spoil your other efforts of grooming well.

## Accessories for Women and Men

Accessories present a world of opportunities when used correctly, from putting together unrelated pieces to transforming it into an outfit of one's choice. If used wisely, accessories can give a different look and image to your personality.

## Mobile Phone

Do ensure that you understand your phone features and menu well. Mobile phone models today represent your character and your status. Avoid carrying very expensive phones unless it is gifted to you. Changing your phone quite regularly does not make a good impression. Take extra care of your phone; a phone with scratches, overused keys and broken parts does not reflect a good picture of you.

Carry original devices and accessories for your mobile and avoid carrying duplicate accessories.

## Laptop/I-pads/Desktops

Even if your laptop is provided by your company, maintain it as you would maintain your own laptop.

Remember, the laptop will be there forever till the time you remain in the race of the corporate world. It is of utmost importance for you to understand the basics of laptop operations, at least basic troubleshooting. There is no harm in doing a crash course or learning from your colleague; for example, how to fix a printer, what you should do when your laptop hangs, formatting, integrating with OHP, etc. It will give you a competitive edge.

Keep your keyboard and screen clean. Incidentally, on a black screen and keyboard the dust reflects more. It is a sign of carelessness. So before the start of the day, give your laptop a thorough clean.

Desktop files should be well-organised; you should know files and folder management. It is suggested that you should not keep more than fifteen icons on the desktop. Anything more than that looks untidy.

The screensaver on your screen should be soothing and extraordinary. A family photograph or good quotes or exclusive photos are recommended. You should never feel ashamed or embarrassed about your screensaver, rather your colleagues should not be embarrassed by your screensaver. One of our ex-bosses used to keep bikini photographs as a screensaver and we would dread the moment he connected his laptop to an OHP.

All of these rules apply to using your desktop computer as well.

Organise space for charger, data cable, CDs, pen drive, etc. in your laptop bag. Don't keep extra and unnecessary things in your laptop bag. If you travel frequently, ensure that you clean your laptop bag once a week.

**Purse and Wallet**

For women, your purse should not be too gaudy or shiny, although they remain in fashion they are not for boardrooms. The size of the purse should be according to your body size. If you are short, do not carry a big purse even if they are in fashion. Buy a purse of good quality that you can think of placing in front of people without any hesitation. Do have a good collection of purses, changing with dresses, occasions, style, need and impression.

For men there is one mantra – the higher you grow, the thinner your purse. The wallet defines the shape of your back pocket and the fall of your trousers. Don't carry bulky and oversized wallets. Keep very few coins, very important paper/cards in your wallet. Your wallet should not be more than half-an-inch in width. With light trousers avoid keeping your wallet in your pocket. Moreover, if you can manage not keeping a wallet at all, it is also trendy.

Refresh your wallet every week. A bulky wallet in your pocket does not look good and also makes your sitting uncomfortable.

Pay attention to your wallet too. Do not carry a worn-out one. It may not be very trendy and of the best quality available, but it should not be worn-out, or torn from the sides.

**Pen**

Avoid keeping plastic pens. A choice of branded and high quality pens always leaves a better impression with clients and seniors.

Do keep two pens always; one for emergency and one for regular use.

**Perfume**

This is a double-edged sword; the fragrance of the perfume can make people happy or irritated. Be very selective about your perfume. Basically, perfume is for fragrance; so you may keep your choice to citrus or aqua if you're not sure. Avoid strong fragrances and locally made perfumes. Body odour is a put off for one and all. It can be so distracting for the person in front of you that s/he might lose track of a very important aspect of a meeting. So you must control body odour. Spray some deodorant or put some powder in your armpits after your bath. Make this a habit.

## Jewellery

Keep it simple whether it is gold, diamonds or platinum or any other metal. Earrings should not hang beyond half-an-inch length. You may, of course, wear your lovely long earrings on a Friday. Bangles are best avoided as they make a lot of sound. You may wear one or two at the most, if you must. Bracelets are a good alternative to bangles. You may wish to try that. Finger rings are fine but keep them to a minimum. Any ornament that makes a sound (a payal for instance) should not be worn. Big nose-rings are an absolute no–no. Toe rings are totally unobtrusive, so you may wear them happily.

Please do avoid wearing gaudy belts even if it is a part of your outfit. If you need to pin up your hair, make sure you use simple black pins. Matching your hair pins with your outfit may be reserved for parties and outings.

Try as much as possible not to mix gold and silver together. If you are wearing a silver earring, try and wear silver neckwear or none at all. If you wear a gold chain with silver earrings and a gold bracelet, it clashes. Matching can include footwear as well. Silver sandals and golden earrings don't go too well. Caution is required in this area with your handbag also. If your handbag has golden hangings or straps or studs, avoid carrying that with silver earrings and silver sandals for example. Your choice of colour should follow through from head to toe.

For men, never show your gold chain out of your shirt and wear no more than two rings on your fingers. But if you have to wear more due to personal beliefs, use your hands as little as possible for pointing, especially at an audience.

Most important of all is to keep your jewellery clean.

**Car/Bike**

Keep your vehicle dent-free, clean, and scratchless and get it washed regularly.

Keep your car organised; generally, people have a habit of throwing things around in their car and make no effort to remove them. It is embarrassing to clean and organise things in front of people so be prepared just in case you have to pick and drop your colleague or take your client somewhere.

If your car is bigger or more expensive than your senior's car, avoid parking your car next to or close to his/her car. Your promotion is more important than flashing your beautiful car, isn't it?

**Cigarettes**

Remember, smoking is not allowed in offices. If you are a smoker, smoke long cigarettes rather than short ones. Long cigarettes show class.

Do not keep cigarettes in your shirt or trouser pocket. It might leave a tobacco stain that may be impossible to remove. Keep it in your drawer and carry them when you go out for a smoke.

Avoid using a matchbox. Using a lighter shows class and makes a good impression. It is a one time investment to buy a classy lighter rather than plastic ones. You may want to invest in it.

Aways keep the flash level lower and light cigarettes for anyone who asks for it. You display your good manners by doing so.

**Glasses**

Spectacles can change the whole look of your face.

Select the latest design in sober specs. Outdated specs will never blend with your contemporary look and will upset your look completely. Clean specs add to a fresh look. Wash your specs once a day, and if you live in hot weather conditions and have a field job, or ride a bike to office, wash them twice a day.

Keep two to three sets of specs handy with you. Do not wear broken specs.

Sunglasses add glamour to your personality. But badly chosen sunglasses can lower your glamour quotient. Here again, take along a friend who would give you an honest opinion when you're buying sunglasses. We have nothing against buying sunglasses at the traffic signal either, except that there are two cons to it. One, you cannot try it on to see how you look and two, it may damage your eyesight. So, be careful when buying sunglasses off the streets. Men look good with navigator glasses more often than not. So if you are in doubt, you can just pick up a pair of navigators.

All clothes and accessories in the world are beautiful. And it appears better and brighter if the person wears and carries it well. You cannot live without clothes in society, and if such an important part of your life does not get full attention from you then that in itself is a reflection of a casual attitude about life. If you are not attentive towards your sense of dressing, your attitude towards life and career is definitely questionable.

Make yourself good to look at. A great personality like SRK was not born good-looking but is very good to look at. Show enthusiasm in wearing your clothes. They are a permanent part of your personality, give due respect and attention to them; it will certainly pay you back.

With two sessions complete you are by now well equipped with information about some important aspects of corporate life. We first discussed communication and language and now we have finished with dressing up to build brand you. Thus, these two sessions can give you a competitive edge. Once you are ready in these two aspects, you are heading towards fighting the battle of situations and occasions. Your communication and dressing helps attract attention toward you, and then how you deal with other situations will further add value to your class, style and elegance.

An average professional would spend around 30 per cent of the time meeting people, in review meetings, conferences and trainings and workshops. Tiny mistakes you unintentionally make, in public, can ruin your impression for life.

People judge you from a single comment to a gesture. All seniors around you are not older than you in age but may have also met hundreds and thousands of people. Any casualness and carelessness will cost you your impression, which you might not win back for years or you might even risk never winning it. But, at the same time, we urge you to look at these occasions positively and optimistically as it provides you with a platform to build a lasting impression and thereby build a superlative brand you. In the upcoming session we deal with how to carry yourself in meetings, conferences, interactions and reviews, as we complete 70 per cent of your daily impression capsule!

"We believe there should be more meeting rooms than cabins in office; in a corporate world you do not do anything alone. It is always "we"!!"

# Session III

# REVIEWS/MEETINGS/CONFERENCES

In every organisation, all functions are linked to each other. The value chain remains incomplete unless attached to all functions. Since work and key deliverables are linked, it is impossible to complete your job without meeting people. We remember one of our service leaders saying that we need to have more meeting rooms in office rather than cabins. He strongly believed that people should sit in bigger rooms and sit together. You would find work happening at a much faster pace. Even organisational structures are taking shape accordingly in recent times, so that one value chain gets complete focus under a single leader. It has been proven that keeping people together and meeting often is the way to success for any organisation. Organisations make special efforts to keep meeting rooms at comfortable locations within the office so that people feel comfortable while sitting through meetings. Meeting rooms are now made with better infrastructure and a good view (if possible), soothing interiors and cool colour combinations so that teams can sit for long hours without any disturbances. When corporates are paying so much attention to minute details of the comfort level of a meeting, it is of utmost importance to hold productive meetings, and you as an organiser or attendee must ensure you add value to every meeting, as well as get the best out of every meeting.

Meetings are one of the most integral parts of a corporate life and of your daily routine. It is also highly impacting and can make or break your efforts at a particular job. There are various aspects that will help make or break your situation, here we will touch upon only one aspect, the behavioural aspect. This aspect is as highly impacting as your flowcharts, trends and data analysis. How you conduct a meeting or participate in a review gives you an opportunity to showcase yourself to a larger audience.

During the above, you will find yourself in two different situations. You will either be conducting any of the events mentioned or attending them. So, we've covered both conducting and attending events in this session, as your attitude needs to be different in both of these situations.

## Conducting a Meeting

A formal invitation or official communication is a must for organised meetings. This invitation has to be sent well in advance. The five-point information is the basic information every participant would require before they are invited for a meeting. Please ensure you mention the objective of the meeting followed by agenda, time and venue, along with information about the other participants of the meeting. This will help participants prepare the relevant information and data that they may require for the meeting. It is always advisable to remind participants about the meeting through an email a day in advance, and an SMS a few minutes in advance (if participants are in the same office). If for any reason the meeting is delayed or cancelled, ensure you inform all the participants immediately.

### Reaching on Time

You have to value time, before time values you. Everything in life is a give and take, so not only should you value your time; you need to value others' time as well. To reach right on time or even a little ahead of time is very important. You don't want people waiting just for you to start a meeting, and then call your cell every two minutes to remind you that they are all waiting for you and vice versa. Making a grand or late entry to a party may be looked upon as a matter of style, but not so for meetings. Nowadays late entry into parties are also no longer considered stylish. It is imperative that you are on time, every time, everywhere. Especially when you have your seniors seated and attending the same event. If you are conducting a meeting, you have to be at the venue at least ten minutes before time to see to the arrangements. If you are attending a meeting, make sure you are out at the gate a minute before meeting time. Just in case you are getting late, inform the concerned person and also your boss, so that they can start the meeting without delay.

### Ensuring Readiness for a Meeting

It would be rather foolish on your part to get ready with your meeting requirements when the participants are already seated.

All requirements for the meeting have to be supervised by you personally if you have called for a meeting. Please remember that if you have done well and organised your material well in advance, you have a better possibility of having a fruitful meeting. Participants may not notice or mention how well-prepared you are for the meeting, but they will not fail to notice if you aren't. This simply makes way for people to pass comments about your organising capabilities. So if you are conducting a meeting, make sure you take the responsibility of being ready.

Once you are ready with your presentation, it is wise to browse through it and look at it from your audience's point of view. You will then definitely have a better idea of what questions may come your way and carry extra data with you accordingly.

Never go to any meeting empty-handed; carrying your laptop or pad and pen is a must.

### How to Start a Meeting

You will always start a meeting by welcoming everybody and with a thank-you note. If there is a delay or any absentees, it is better to mention the reason for the delay and the reason for not attending the meeting by the respective participants. If you are informed about any participant running late, you are not expected to be sarcastic but to be silent. But be apologetic on their behalf for a delayed start. While conducting a meeting, you are the person who has something to say/discuss. So you must take complete ownership of the meeting. If there are people who don't know each other, then you should organise a round of introductions. Introduce yourself first and then you may pick a person sitting at one end of the table and invite him/her to introduce themselves, and then go on to the next person and so on. Normally, if there is a very senior person present, though some of the participants may not know him/her, you must let that introduction pass first. Then you may request for everyone's focus on the presentation that you have and start.

It is extremely important to state clear objectives for the meeting and what is expected out of the participants.

Do mention the flow of meeting along with expected time to finish. If you are sure, give a specific time, or else mention that it depends on the participants. If you are attending a meeting, please follow the basic rules of the meeting. Give a 100 per cent to the meeting and do not disturb other meeting participants, avoid taking calls or leaving frequently and coming back to the meeting room. Keeping your phone on meeting mode by default should be your own rule.

If you are asked to introduce yourself, start with your name and what work you are currently handling. That should do. Make it brief and smart.

For example, 'I am Vijay and am currently handling Corporate Sales.' It is enough unless you are asked for more.

## Prescribing Important Rules for the Meeting

It is recommended to mention the rules of the meeting, if any. Right at the beginning please do mention that questions at any point of time are always welcome, and that participants must feel free to raise a question. But then there might be a pest in the meeting, trying to prove his/her 'intelligence', and will butt in every now and then with questions. This sometimes interrupts the flow of your presentation. In this case you may politely mention that any questions could be saved for later, till you complete what you're saying, as more often than not, most questions people have in mind are normally answered alongside the presentation.

## DURING MEETINGS

### Handling the Flow

In case there is a difference of opinion during the meeting you are conducting, under no circumstances is it advisable to raise your voice or even frown. Take all that comes to you in your stride and move along. If there are questions that you do not have an answer to right then, it is all right to mention that you will check into the matter and get back to the concerned. But then, if you say this at every point, your audience may lose interest in your meeting as they may find that you aren't on top of what you are presenting.

How to make a presentation interesting again is a totally different aspect, which is highly impacting; we will not be getting into the details of presentation skills because most of the presentation skills are covered under different sessions in this book, like how to speak, dress, etc. But there are some important dos and don'ts which are a must to keep in mind while presenting. There is a lot of help on the internet and also books written on this subject, which we recommend that you read.

Your presentation should be in a flow starting from objectives, background of objectives, etc., depending on the topic you are covering. Your slides should be as simple as possible and should not have long sentences. All points should be in bullet points, which you are expected to speak about and explain. Each slide should contain the outcome of the slide especially when you are presenting data. Using a font of equal size and style, and pleasing colours keeps your audiences' attention on the subject rather than distracting from your slides. Adding sounds to slides is not recommended, unless you have to show a video clip. Using picture and clip art is impressive if used intelligently. Try and learn the powerpoint application really well. Displaying some unique features of powerpoint through presentation is creating a silent impression.

Adding a bit of humour every now and then keeps your audience in good spirits and also portrays you as a pleasant personality. But don't overdo it. Keep in mind that after all, it is a formal meeting.

Pay full attention to what's being said even if it doesn't interest you much. Even if the presenter is very boring and you feel like the topic is the 'lullaby of the century', you must pay attention. You never know, in that boring topic you may find something that will really help you do your job better. Constantly fiddling with your cellphone is an absolute no-no. You may want to look at your messages and missed calls, but do it during intervals. The best bet is to turn it upside down and look at it every twenty minutes or so.

Asking questions is good. You get to clear your doubts. But ask questions only to clear your doubts, not to get extra mileage out of it, thinking it makes you look intelligent to be able to ask questions. It does, no doubt, but only if you ask relevant questions. Otherwise you will be looked at as a pest. Relevance again is another thing. Whatever you have in mind, is most often relevant of course, but you will find that there are some doubts you can clarify by yourself, by giving the presenter enough time to take you through the entire topic. Try to find an answer by yourself first. It works best to save your question to the end of the meeting.

When tea/coffee and cookies are served, do not gulp down all the cookies kept in front of you. One or at the most two is what you should take. While drinking water, it is best to pour water into a glass and drink it. However, there might be situations where you only have a small bottle kept, in which case you must be careful not to make too much noise while gulping down the water. Drink gracefully; small sips would help you achieve that.

If you have a cold, make sure the box of tissues is close to you. Blowing into tissues in front of people is very disgusting for them. Just clean up enough without making any noise. If you have to blow your nose, excuse yourself and head to the restroom. The same goes for sneezing bouts or coughing spells!

**Managing Breaks**

During lunch or breaks, get to know the other participants, if they are not already known to you. Catch up with them, or make those pending calls and send all your SMSes. One of the challenges you face during breaks is that everyone wants a break on time but it is difficult to manage to get everyone back into the meeting room on time. The rule of thumb is to get seniors back on time and the rest will follow.

### After a Meeting

Ensure that you go through the points you have concluded in the meeting and the points pending for action. Ensure every pending action has the name of the person responsible for completing the same. Ensuring a timeline for completion is also very important. If you are attending a meeting, please do mention action items you are taking with you from your end. It is better to mention this at the end of the meeting so as to provide clarity about tasks entrusted and ownerships taken. We are sure the people concerned will certainly add value to your points, if relevant.

If it is a training session, when you are asked for feedback at the end of the session, make it honest and to the point so that the trainers can actually take away some value from your feedback and improve their training. Mention the good things too, so that they continue with them in their sessions to come.

Do send 'minutes of the meeting' to all members of the meeting along with their respective seniors. Minutes of the meeting should certainly have a by-whom and by-when column. End of the day work has to be done and it is better to keep members posted on points pending and allocated to get the best out of your meeting. Unfortunately, in the most professional atmosphere also, you have to keep reminding people for action pending by them. The first reminder has to be verbal or can be a polite mail if many people are involved. The second should be by mail, and the third should go with cc (copy) to seniors.

Also mention the members who have completed action on their points, for silent comparison. The fourth reminder onwards, please walk down to his/her senior and your senior, and let the action happen.

After all, the purpose of the meeting is to put across your points and get the work done from the respective people concerned.

## Meeting a Client or Guest

Any wait beyond five minutes is not appreciated if you have given a fixed time to someone. Do keep the concerned person informed if you are getting late due to an unexpected emergency. In this scenario, it is recommended that you speak to the person directly rather than passing a message through a receptionist or security guards.

Show appreciation if your client or guest has reached on time and enquire if they had any problem finding the office. It is important that at the time of finalising a meeting with your guest that you explain in detail, with a landmark, about your office location and special instructions of any kind like car parking, visitor check by security guards, etc.

If you have planned to meet on a Friday or Saturday, it is better to dress formally for the meeting. There are certain things which 'if you do not do, people will notice; and if you do them, people will not notice.'

Sometimes meetings take place outside your office. Or you may have to visit another office to meet a client. While visiting another office, be sure to be on your best behaviour. Follow all the rules laid down by that office, like signing in, taking a visitors tag, waiting at the reception, etc. Do not argue with the security guard or receptionist about any policy they may have about visitors. There is also no need to strike up a friendship or make conversation with the receptionist. Just do as you are told and follow every rule meticulously. It's always better to arrive a few minutes early, especially if it's the first time you are visiting that office. Acting over-familiar and too much at home is considered naïve and is unacceptable. You can't be casual, formality is the key here. If there are magazines and newspapers kept on the table, ask for permission before you pick them up to read. Otherwise utilise your cellphone. Send SMSes and catch up with friends and family. Look busy and occupied. These are some times in life, when the cell seems like a boon.

Similarly, when you receive a visitor in your office, inform the security or receptionist in advance about the upcoming visit. Then follow all the necessary dos and don'ts we have mentioned previously about conducting a meeting.

## REVIEWS

### Conducting a review

If you are conducting a review, send the review intimation well in advance so that your team members have enough time to prepare for it. A soft reminder just a day before the review would be welcome by your team. If it is a regular monthly or weekly affair, you may as well have a scheduled time and day. It also helps if you tell employees in advance what it is that you are looking to review. A presentation format or the topics that you want them to cover would help them a great deal and will also make the review more productive. Stick to the time slated for the review as much as possible. Postponing it often makes it lose its steam and the team feels offended. They may feel that you do not value their time, and inconvenienced as they need to keep updating the data every time you postpone it.

Besides you being more knowledgeable on your subject, your team also expects you to add value to their work. It pays to remember that reviews are not only about pointing out to your team members what they have done wrong, and how they have not lived up to your expectations. It's also about giving them guidance and helping them achieve what they haven't been able to achieve by themselves.

If it is a long review, make sure you arrange for refreshments. A hearty lunch after a review or in between, is something most team members would look forward to. It also gives you a chance to unwind with the team, after an intense review session. While at lunch it is best not to discuss what happened in the review, or anything remotely related to it. If there are still things to discuss, you may as well extend the time by a couple of hours more and get it over with, within the meeting room itself.

A bit of laughter here and there lightens up the atmosphere and puts everyone at ease. This has to be initiated by you. The team members would be too occupied with what they have to say, to be able to pull in that bit of laughter.

If your key deliverable requires an intense target orientation, it is well-accepted to put your point across with aggression. Everyone has a different style and smart people are aggressive without raising their voice. Being abusive, personal and raising one's voice beyond a limit is not appreciated. Your team will only pretend to respect you but never really will.

### Attending a Review

Be prepared. There is no compromise to this aspect. Be completely on top of what you are presenting. Know much more than what you have displayed in your slides. If your junior has helped you prepare your presentation (which is all right), sit with that person and go through each and every detail with that person. Leave nothing to chance. Carry enough data, whether or not you think you might require it. It's always better to be over-equipped than under-equipped. Try and gather all the answers and carry them with you. Though it's all right not to have ALL the answers right then, how often you use the phrase, 'I'll get back to you with this', is important. Uttering this phrase too often, as a response to every second question posed to you, would automatically make your seniors think that you are not involved enough, or not sincere enough in your work.

However, if you really aren't prepared it's best to say so candidly. Beating around the bush and answering a question with irrelevant answers is even worse. That leaves an everlasting impression and it's often very hard to shake that off. First and foremost, be honest to yourself and the person in front of you.

If there is something that has not been done, please mention it. Along with it, also mention how you are going to turn around the situation, what your plan is, and by when one can expect to see that turnaround. What support you require to do so must also be specified. It's really okay to say that you are lost and you need guidance. But you can only do that when you have sincerely tried all your options and failed.

Avoid arguments unless you are extremely sure you will emerge a winner. Even if the argument falls flat and neither of you gain the stronghold, since you are the presenter you will be the loser. It will not only disturb you and disrupt your thinking, but will also make the atmosphere tense, and this will not work in your favour.

If it is a regular review it is recommended to start the review with action points raised in the last meeting along with action taken. It opens the review on a good note and also brings up any pending issues and concerns, and is a good opportunity to share if any support is required. This will also reflect your seriousness and the attention you paid during the meeting.

## CONFERENCES

### Large Conferences

Conferences are as good as marriage functions at home and need detailed planning and excellence in execution. Conferences could be within the organisation, across organisations, across countries and even open for the public. Managing and organising a conference requires event-management skills.

### Organising a Conference

When you are ready with the agenda, date and venue of the conference, you are ready for the next step of sending out the invitation. A formal invitation or official communication is a must for conferences. This invitation has to be sent well in advance to the participants so as to allow distant participants enough time to plan their travel. This will also help participants to prepare the relevant information and data that they may require for the meeting. The best way is to name a single point of contact (SPOC) for the conference and assign a team member to help him/her to execute the communication work so that it can happen at a fast pace with efficient and equal division of labour.

### Communication, Planning and Events

It is advisable to keep all participants well informed. Generally, it is easy to jot down the kind of information visitors or members may require about the conference and location and intimate them in advance. They may like an update about accommodation, the route to the location, weather, dress code, etc. Please provide all of these well in advance.

The SPOC should organise a helpdesk or site to pose questions, if any. If it is a smaller group conference, make best use of SMS group messaging.

The agenda and venue specifications should be handed over at the time of arrival or along with conference kit, if any. Any specially designed dress code should be kept well in advance in the participants' respective rooms.

### During and After the Conference

It is always better to send a reminder to all the participants before the start of the meeting or event. The menu for lunch and dinner should be planned according to visitors' preferences. A written thank-you note along with a local souvenir to carry home as a remembrance of the conference, is appreciable. Keeping a check after all the members have reached home and enquiring after them is a much appreciated gesture and is sure to win some good words for you and for the overall organisation of the conference.

Attending a conference is covered in the session 'Official Travelling'.

**Appraisal Meeting**

Appraisal meetings will always remain the most important meeting for anyone. A few companies do this quarterly, a few do it twice a year and some have an annual meeting. Some of them don't do a quantitative appraisal at all and simply appraise you on your face value.

You will come across a few companies who go purely by quantitative measures on your key performance areas/indicators and rate you based on your achievements in each area. But the climax and future of all employees lie in the bell curve. Most companies use the bell curve as a model to rate their employees' performances. We will not dwell on what a 'bell curve' is, but you should know that it is basically a complete excel exercise. And the boss has to come up with a bell curve no matter what. In order to enable your boss to come up with a good bell curve, shuffle of ratings happens in seconds for your full year performance. (So worship the bell curve. Just kidding!)

Nevertheless, an appraisal meeting gives you an opportunity to know what your boss feels about you and indicates to you your strengths and weaknesses with an objective to get the best out of you. As an employee you must keep a few important things in mind while getting ready for an appraisal meeting.

Fill your self-appraisal form with utmost sincerity and dedication. It does not matter whether your boss reads it or not, you must do your part. It is a simple exercise for you because you are the best person to list down where you stand against your key responsibilities. Read and understand the process thoroughly before you fill the form. Contact the concerned person if you have any doubt in understanding it. Go through the rating calculation and read your appraisal form thoroughly. Attaching relevant data and documents is important but do not attach anything which is not relevant. Don't worry about it being too lengthy if all the information you have added is important. This shows your seriousness towards your appraisal activity and also creates an impression about your seriousness towards your job.

Make notes for your meeting. If you are a boss, make notes for your team. If you are to be appraised make them for yourself too. There are some general questions that are asked during the appraisal meeting, like – How has your year been? What are the challenges you faced? How do you like the culture of the organisation? What are your plans for next year? What do you need to improve upon and what do you feel about the appraisal process per se?

For the boss it is important to discuss Key Performance Indicators (KPIs) point by point. Do give personal feedback too, such as what you like about him/her and what you don't. Most importantly, keep handy references of incidents during the year. If your boss does not give you personal feedback, you can ask for it.

Keep your mind open during the meeting. Take feedback positively. Don't bring out any points of argument while feedback is being given. Should you have any clarifications, you may make them after your boss has given you the feedback. One of the important situations in life where your attitude comes to the fore is during feedback – how you handle and take feedback and your reaction thereafter.

Ensure the meeting is well-organised without any disturbance at all. You may hang a note outside your room stating 'No disturbance' or 'Appraisal meeting going on'. The associates involved in operations and scheduling generally organise these meetings on weekends or late evenings to avoid disturbance. Keep your phone on silent mode and upside down so that you cannot even see the screen. All team members should be told in advance about the specific time for the meeting so that there is ample time to prepare for it.

## Reward and Recognition Functions

This is by far one of the most integral parts of the corporate world. Keeping everyone and ourselves motivated is very important for high quality delivery at work. Recognising the performers and making them feel good about themselves and motivating the non-performers to be able to be in that position the next time around helps a great deal.

If you are the person giving out the rewards, you are expected to speak a few words before the function actually begins. So go prepared. Make your speech brief but highly impacting and encouraging. We would suggest talking about how the business has been so far and share some facts and figures of the business that are positive and encouraging. Then of course mention without fail, that without the best efforts of this crowd in front of you, it wouldn't have been possible. It's important to smile a lot in these occasions, and you are expected to set the trend.

While giving out the certificates or prizes, make sure to look in the eyes of the person receiving the award, give a firm handshake and a big smile of course. 'Congratulations' or 'Keep it up' should do for the words that you need to speak while presenting the award.

Dress extra well on this day as you will be the centre of attraction. All eyes will be focused on you and for a long period of time. Photographs may be taken and placed in the office album. So dress accordingly.

Announcing impromptu prizes for a performance during this function is a great way to connect to the team. Or, if it's not a big function, announcing a lunch/dinner with the winners also makes a great impact.

While accepting a reward again, look in the eyes of the person presenting it to you, give a firm handshake and your big smile of course (this would naturally be there as you are the hero of the day!). Again, dress extra cautiously today. Don't compromise on that.

If you have any talent such as singing or dancing, be sure to take part in the function, if there is one. Don't be shy about it. This is a great opportunity for you to showcase your talent which otherwise may not be known to anyone. And, trust us; people remember the performance and the performers for a long time. So go ahead and participate. It's a good chance for you to be noticed.

## Town Hall/Open Forum

Some call it 'Town Hall', some call it 'Open Forum'. Basically, it is a platform for employees to clarify their doubts and ask questions to their seniors about things that are playing on their minds. It's not very often that you get to meet the entire senior management together, and also not very often that you get a chance to clarify your doubts. So take this opportunity to come out with what's on your mind and get your answers. But please remember to ask only very relevant questions – questions that will concern most of the audience, if not all. Mamata has an episode from her life in this regard. The organisation that she was with had a six day working week. Everybody would crave a two day weekend, but none would ask for it. Then they decided to have an open forum every month. She took this opportunity to ask when employees would get a five day working week. Month after month she would ask the same question only to hear that no progress has been made in that direction. Then finally after several months it was declared, 'Yes – it will be a five day working week going forward.' The joy in the auditorium is hard to describe. Everyone came and congratulated her; some thanked her, as if she had made that decision. So you see, when you ask relevant questions, the impact can be huge. Please shoot your questions when you are given that opportunity.

While taking questions in an open forum, it's very important to keep an open mind and to be non-judgmental. Otherwise people will sense that you make judgments about the questions they ask and thereby would stop asking questions. That could mean the end of having an open forum and addressing your team's grievances. In one of the forums we had, an employee posed a HR policy question to the HR Head. Apparently what was asked for was already there, which the person wasn't aware of. Instead of taking it in her stride the HR Head commented that 'Ignorance is not an excuse for asking questions in open forums'. That was not all. The HR Head also went back and mailed all HR policies to that person, disregarding whether it was related to the question or not. Not only was the person who had asked the question extremely disheartened by this entire episode, but also, her entire friend circle in office stopped asking any questions during an open forum. This is detrimental to the growth of a healthy organisation. These are also things that we must keep in mind while taking questions.

Also, you may not have an answer ready, to which you may give a time frame by when you will get back with an answer. And, please stick to that time. Otherwise you will fail to gain the confidence of people.

### Training Programmes

Training, for most people is taken as an official holiday. You have to understand for life that any training is not a pastime and it should be taken with full dedication and an open mind, just like your day-to-day job. It is not right to say that training is only required for customer-facing jobs and at lower levels, training at every level and age in your career is a must; as one has to keep brushing up on their learning and skills. A successful professional like Jack Welch still likes to attend training programmes as he believes that learning is never-ending. No one can claim to know any subject so completely that one does not need any training. If one does that, s/he has blocked him/herself from any further improvement in his/her personal and professional life.

You cannot expect to take 100 per cent from a training programme, but if you are able to take some lessons from every training, which you make use of in your personal and professional life, that is a successful training for you. Even if it is the second or third time you have been asked to attend the same training, do attend with full spirits and an open mind. Either you have something more to learn or you can brush up on your existing knowledge.

In a training programme you also need to participate. Many trainers keep an award for 'Best Participant' as they have found that learning is much better with participation. Mamata had won once and she was delighted. She had won a photo frame where she now keeps her daughter's picture. Humans, by nature are competitive, hence even winning a 'Best Participant' award keeps us motivated.

Blend yourself in with the ambience and atmosphere. Work as a team during workshops and trainings. Give everybody else a chance to put across their points of view. Give in your inputs definitely, but do not expect your every point to be appreciated and accepted.

Remember from what you have learned, it is you who is going to benefit later, not the organisation who has put you through the training. What you have learnt will become part of your personality and the skills you acquire will help you forever. It's yours to use, whenever you need it. Knowledge is like sand, you never know when it will turn into gold. Keep learning all the time and from anyone, anywhere!

Meetings, conferences and training programmes generally make you tense. At every step of your career, no matter what stage you are in and what level you are at, there is always an anxiety before any such performance and it is believed that if you are not nervous, you have not prepared yourself for the best. And, that nervousness remains till the meetings, conferences or trainings are concluded; so organisations make sure that you do not carry this home and ensure that they organise gatherings for lighter moments to change your mood. That's when parties and gatherings come into the picture. But, that is not the end of your presentation; you are only getting ready for your next performance. Such parties and gatherings give you a whole lot of opportunities to present yourself well and if you are not careful, it might overshadow all the good work you may have done. So, take a deep breath and get-set-ready to be a party animal and a complete professional, both at the same time, in our next session: party time!

'People who enjoy themselves the most are the people who work the most.'

# Session IV

# PARTY TIME

Till now we have been discussing the situations which are related to your work. You are judged on reactions, gestures and behaviour related to work occasions. You are expected to be formal – in both clothes and attitude. When it comes to a party, you are expected to be casual in respect to clothing and even in behaviour. Once you have demonstrated your style in dressing, as well as words coupled with manners to leave an impression and have gained skill in your official/professional style, it's time for you to demonstrate the other side of you. If you need to be reserved and have an introverted kind of personality in professional dealings, you get a chance to be a real party animal and to demonstrate the other side of your nature during parties. Please remember why parties are organised by companies. The sole objective of parties is to enjoy, mix with colleagues/clients who you otherwise may not deal with on a day-to-day basis in your work assignments, and represent you as a situational person. You cannot afford to be quiet and aloof in parties. You have to be part of the enjoyment and make the best use of such opportunities. Yes, parties are opportunities! First, to get to know people apart from work and vice versa. Second, you demonstrate your actual likes and dislikes. Third, your chance to share your wisdom other than your work-knowledge and also gain knowledge from others on other affairs. Last but not the least, you can dress up for the occasion as your sense of style tells you.

As we have shared during the earlier sessions, opinions are made in parties as well. If you are sophisticated in your professional dealings then you have to be elegant in parties too, yet, participative. It's a bit of a tricky situation. You cannot be reserved and formal, yet cannot let your hair down completely, and make a fool of yourself. More importantly, you cannot lose all the respect and admiration you may have gained professionally. We remember an incident of a very good hard-working colleague, who joined the party and had to be taken home within one hour of the party as he drank like a fish and within no time, he was out of control. He could not control himself and started throwing up. Just imagine what he did to himself. He not only spoiled an opportunity but also disturbed the whole atmosphere for everyone else. Would you like to join parties with such colleagues in future? No, you would avoid them. Not only that, you would also tend to disregard the hard and smart work that he normally delivers then on. We remember how much fun his office friends made of him over the months thereafter. He was embarrassed and avoided standing in groups. This is just one example of how one may lose their impression.

Nowadays, with such hectic schedules and stressful jobs, most professional organisations use parties, get-togethers and outings as a remedy to freshen up employees and moreover, they gain by allowing them to become friendly and close to each other. Business runs on relationships and such gatherings are brilliant opportunities to gain the best in work and business.

If you happen to be part of an army culture, you would know that attending parties are as important as attending office. And this stands true for both single invitations as well as family invitations. It is a matter of discipline for every level in the army. The objective is the same – work together and enjoy together. In the corporate world, parties are not always mandatory, they are without any compulsion. Generally, it is left to your convenience to attend. Being disciplined in attending parties reflects that you do not just mean business, you mean relationships also. There are examples where some colleagues have surprised others in such gatherings by their recreational skills. And such activities gain attention as well as attract colleagues towards you. Otherwise, who would ever know that you play the guitar, can sing, write poems, are good at mimicry or have any other art in you.

Parties are as important as professional meetings, you are not only expected to be regular in attending parties but also participative in them. Before we discuss parties it is very important to talk about attending parties first. Only once you are convinced about attending them can we discuss how to make an everlasting impression outside work. Creating an impression on the professional front is only half the job done. To be a complete professional, you cannot afford to miss such opportunities.

If you are attending a party and sitting in a corner with only your close friends, you have made a good attempt by attending, and would get full marks for that. But, you have still not utilised the opportunity to make other friends and get to know them beyond work. It is said that the British are very reserved by nature, they always wait for the other person to come and introduce themselves. They might not initiate talks. On the other hand, it is said that everyone will know an American at a party, because they love to go around and make friends. Both styles have advantages and disadvantages. But, the best style is your natural style, coupled with tips you should pick from the rest of the session.

### Types of Parties

Such gatherings could be of a different nature. It could be a professional or a non-professional party. By professional we mean one that is organised by the organisation with your collegeaues only. And a non-professional party could be organised with office colleagues only but organised by you. Such gatherings could be at home, restaurants, clubs, etc. We should take a note of professional gatherings to start with.

## PROFESSIONAL PARTIES

### Acknowledge Invitation

The first step to start your impression is by acknowledging your invitation. Such an invitation could come to you verbally as well as through non-verbal means. Take the opportunity to thank the inviter for the invitation in case of a verbal invite, even before you get to know the reason for the party. Please show your instant reaction of happiness on receiving such an invitation. If the invitation comes to you through mail, acknowledge it with a note of thanks by confirming your presence. If the invitation is from a group ID where a reply can be sent, do try to find out who the concerned person is, to convey your thanks. If in any scenario, you are not able to find the concerned person, wait for the moment to meet them at the venue.

**Be on Time**

Reaching the venue on time might not make your impression in just a single party, but make it a habit to be on time, people will certainly make a note of this. Being on time not only demonstrates discipline but also does not put you in a situation to explain the reason for your late arrival. Even in a big gathering where you feel no one will be bothered about your presence, you would certainly have your own set of friends, whom you would keep waiting. Even if you are doing it for yourself, it is believed that reaching on time brings success to you on time. As we say, value time, time will value you.

**Check the Location of the Venue**

Once you have decided to reach on time, you will certainly make sure you know the location of the venue well in advance. Do check with the person who had sent the invite. Generally, nowadays a location map or a landmark is provided along with the invitation. Do check with your friends. Finding the location in advance will help you plan your timings to start and reach, and will also ensure parking comfort.

## Dress Up for the Occasion

Once you are attending the party, attend with enthusiasm. And, dress for the occasion. There could be two scenarios: either the party invitation will include a dress code or there will be no dress code. In both scenarios, dress for the occasion. The dress code is to be strictly followed and if it's a theme-party dress code, that's an opportunity for you to show your wholehearted participation. If the party is without a dress code, be the real you! Do wear clothes you enjoy wearing other than office favourites. Be sure your clothes are different from your office attire. You can wear casual bright colours, fashionable shirts, stylish accessories like a belt, watch, sandals/shoes, purse, glasses, etc. You can change your hairstyle, use gel and just be yourself.

## Make your Presence Felt

Go out and meet friends and colleagues all around, both who you know and don't know. Do make it a point to greet your immediate seniors at an appropriate time. It is all the more important if it is a family gathering. Take your spouse/partner around and introduce him/her to your friends and their spouses/partners, just in case they have not met before. Take your family to your immediate seniors and introduce them. Before you introduce them to your seniors, do tell your spouse/partner about the person s/he is going to meet and the position s/he handles. It might be embarrassing for you just in case your spouse/partner is not able to catch the correct name while wishing them.

### Official Talks

Even if you are the senior most in a party or you are part of a party, do not initiate official talks – unless it is organised with business partners, for business discussions. You have to develop the art of talking about things other than work. You can talk about current affairs, weather, recent good and bad experiences and if you are aware of the other person's favourite topic, talk about that. We will be discussing this a little more in detail in the last session. You can also take this opportunity to gain knowledge on subjects which interest you.

### Drinks

It is said that if you are good friends you drink together. Drinking is not a bad habit if it is occasional and with groups only. You are possibly developing a bad habit of drinking if you have started drinking alone. If you have not been drinking, it is not recommended to test your drinking skills in parties with seniors, unless it is forced on you due to some rituals of the function.

It is extremely important to know your limits of drinking, whatever brand or type of drink you prefer, like beer, whisky, vodka, wine, etc. Your limit on the number of pegs or glasses that you can handle well, should be known to you and you must stick to it. If you do not, the moment you realise that it is hitting you beyond your control, keep your glass aside. Remember, hard drinks or even strong beer sometimes gives a good knock all of a sudden and might not be slow in intoxication. If you feel a little out of control, go to the washroom and pass urine, wash your face with a good amount of water and join the party and avoid drinking anymore or drink very slowly. After every peg you finish, it's a good idea to have a glass of plain water, just like you'd have had a peg of alcohol.

Gaining good knowledge on liquor is a very good idea. The type of liquor, how and where they are produced, and which brands are good brands, will add value to your discussion, if any. Buy a book on liquor and update yourself. It is a very interesting subject and we promise you, you would love reading it. Make it a point to read one anyway; it is educational, whether you drink or not.

Do you know why whisky and brandy glasses are different shapes and sizes? Do you know why a red wine glass and a white wine glass have different stems? Knowing about the types of tumblers and which tumbler goes with which liquor is also a very interesting topic. All these topics have scientific reasons behind them and have developed over the years, and have been followed religiously and you better not goof up on the same if you are given the responsibility of handling the bar in a friendly party. Red wine is taken at room temperature, so the glass stem is short. This is because even if your hand touches the glass, your body heat will not affect the temperature of red wine. Similarly, white wine is taken chilled and so the glass has a longer stem, so that your hand does not touch the glass and your wine remains chilled for a longer time. If you have noticed, brandy glasses have a very small stem with a very big scoop, because brandy is supposed to be taken with hot water. Would you like to know why the brandy balloon tumbler is shaped so? When you study liquor, that book should also explain to you the beauty and science of using different tumblers for different liquor.

Knowing the regular names of cocktails and mocktails will help you place your order according to your choice. How to open a champagne bottle and a cork of wine and with which tool, if it is known, your hand-picked knowledge now will become gold anyday. Become familiar with this subject; even if you don't drink.

Over drinks, if you are not talking business, one good option is to crack jokes and find a reason to laugh together. These days life is so easy that you get SMS jokes every now and then on your mobile, and occasionally it so happens that when it is time for jokes, you tend to forget them. Keeping selective jokes in a favourite folder of your phone is recommended. Remember when you are telling a joke or a story, you get 100 per cent attention of the group around. So, having some selected and uncommon jokes will help you lead the group or be participative at least. And what have you achieved? You have made more friends. Though the art of telling a joke is natural, you should keep one thing in mind – dragging a joke a bit longer will make it lose its charm. So be crisp and to the point. Soon practice will make you a master.

### Smoking

Thanks to regulations, now you cannot smoke in restaurants and public areas. Smoking in a public area, even if you are sure nobody is watching you or will restrict you, should not be done. Take a break from the group if you feel you have to smoke. Smoke in an area recommended by the management or owners. You must be more conscious about it after you are three-four drinks down. We have covered some smoke-related manners in another session as well, which we do not wish to repeat here. All of that holds good here as well.

**Dance**

Dance even if you do not know how to dance. You do not have to be a professional to go to the floor. Dance is whatever you do on the floor, it becomes your style of dancing. Make sure you dance within your limits and maintain professional protocol even on the floor. Dancing without control and hitting people around on the floor can take your impression away in seconds. Avoid provocative movements and just swing to the tune that is playing.

This one is for the guys. Do not be over-enthusiastic to dance with the girls. Ensure you do not force the ladies around to dance with you. They will come to you and dance with you on their own if you behave decently and are under control. Getting too close for comfort will ensure that no girl dances with you. We have covered bad breath and body odour, etc., in another session. Do take care of those aspects as well if you wish to have a good dance partner for the evening.

**Dinner**

Once you have come for a party, do not be in a hurry unless you have already informed your hosts about any exigency in advance. Ladies are expected to start dinner on time and men are expected to follow or join them only when they start. Follow the protocol, should there be any in the party you are attending. If there isn't any particular protocol being followed, just be sensitive about letting the ladies and the seniors start dinner first. Ladies are generally expected to ensure kids are served before they start. Join your group of friends for dinner together and wait for each person to finish their drinks before you proceed for dinner.

If it is a buffet-style arrangement (which most parties are these days), please stand in a queue and do not barge in from the wrong side. Be quick in deciding what you want to eat, you are not expected to stand and think about what to take and what not to. Don't stand around trying to pick and choose your favourite non-vegetarian pieces of meat, digging into the serving dish, while the others are standing behind you in the queue. Pick up the ladle, serve yourself and place the ladle back in a convenient position for the next person to use. Do not serve yourself with your hands even if it is a dry item. Use the serving spoon provided.

After drinks, try and find a place to sit, even if it means sitting on a parapet wall. You tend to drop food onto your clothes otherwise. When you are drunk, sitting would give you a good hold over your plate of food. Make sure your chewing noise is not audible to anyone around. This leaves a bad impression. And don't get caught licking your fingers even if the food is extremely tasty.

Make proper use of a paper/cloth napkin and clean your mouth properly. Gargling and gulping water at places where people are eating is a bad habit. Make as little noise as possible while eating and while washing up thereafter. Please do not blow your nose into cloth napkins. If you must do so, ask for paper tissues. Cloth napkins are only meant to protect your clothes from food or for wiping your mouth. So, open up the cloth napkin provided and lay it gently on your lap. If any cutlery or napkin falls on the ground, do not pick it up for further use. Call the waiter for a replacement.

### Leaving the Party

Do not scoot out of a party. Do inform all concerned, especially seniors, before you leave. Do not skip or show off the speed of your bike or car, when you are drunk. Ask if anyone wants a lift.

### Confirmation Courtesy

If you are concerned about anyone in the party reaching home safe, especially ladies or a drunken friend, do make it a point to make a call or SMS them to confirm.

## PERSONAL PARTIES

Personal parties can be either organised at home or outside.

### Tips for Home Parties for Invitees

If you are invited to a home party, do carry some gift or present for the person, if the occasion is known. If it is without any occasion, carry some souvenirs or flowers for the ladies, or a box of chocolates for kids at home, or a bottle of wine.

Please be sensitive about the culture of your host, South and West Indians might prefer to keep footwear outside their home. There is no harm to check with your host what they prefer. Do not roam around the house all by yourself, unless invited by your host to show yourself around. Do pick something to compliment about their home decorations, kids' manners, etc. Do pay a compliment about the food. Your hosts have been busy throughout the day planning and arranging for the gathering for sure. It is important to give positive comments, but be honest. Use the complimenting skills that we spoke about in one of the earlier sessions.

Mind your sitting posture; and remember to keep things back in the same place and in proper order or where you picked them up from. If you have taken cushions for rest they should be placed back properly when you get up.

If you are invited with family, ensure each one of them are given a proper introduction. If your kids have been playing in their kids' room, ensure your kids place all the toys back in order. Make sure your kids are under your radar, and do not let them touch and play with things kept for decoration. Hosts may not like to say 'no' to your kids but you should be the one to take charge of them and control them. Your kids should have food in your presence, so that they do not litter food here and there. Extraordinarily naughty kids need extra attention.

### Being a Host

As a host, you should ensure that each invitee is well looked after. Every guest must be offered every snack that is served around, and you must keep an eye on your guests' drink glasses.

Everytime your guests' glass is empty you must ask, 'May I refresh your glass?' Hosts must offer to show their guests around their home.

Hosts need to ensure food arrangement for non-vegeterian and vegetarian people. All vegetarians should be well informed about all vegetarian snacks and food. Place them separately in two different corners of the table so that there is no ambiguity.

Hosts should try to give return gifts to all kids even if there isn't any occasion for the party. This is an extremely good gesture. It may not be possible every time, but if it is possible, do ensure it. Some chocolates and candies would also do.

Organising parking well in advance for all invitees is another additional gesture you can make. These days, apartment complexes do not allow guest parking or they have arranged guest parking spots. It's the duty of the hosts to inform all invitees in advance about the location of your home and parking lot. Keeping security guards informed well in advance about the arrival of your guests will ensure that they have been looked after without any hassles.

Do call and thank all guests for their gifts and mention what you got from them the next day. In some cultures, it is important to open gifts in front of everyone. Generally, it does not go well with the Indian culture. So be cautious about doing the right thing here.

Pay extra attention to your home on the day of the party. Get some fresh flower arrangements. Make sure you have a variety of liquor available. Stock up on napkins and tissues. Make your cutlery and crockery sparkling clean. Lay the table well, even if it is a buffet-style arrangement.

## Dinner with a Client

The first thing to remember here is to take your client to a place you are familiar with. Don't get adventurous while choosing a place when it comes to taking your client out. Be very choosy about the venue, select the best within your budget and let the location be more convenient to the client than you.

If you are the host, keep your client informed about what kind of meal it is. Buffet, restaurant sitting, bar-style or nightclub. Make reservations beforehand so the experience is smooth. Inform your client about the timing so that both parties reach there on time. Be wary of the fact that a table is reserved for you during the restaurant's peak business hours, which means if you do not you show up or show up late, it's a loss of business for the restaurant. Respect other people's businesses as you respect yours. The beauty of a business meal is that none of your client's team members should feel out of place. It is extremely important for you to involve them in some sort of discussion, to keep them participative. The more you keep them involved, the better the comment they will make about the meeting.

Do keep control over the food and drinks being served to them and make sure they are served before you are served. You have to pass instructions to the restaurant staff in advance to give more attention to them. But do not be very pushy with food and drinks, more than it is required. Ordering is normally the host's duty; however, if you feel you are comfortable asking around about what to order, depending on the relationship you share, it's all right to ask your guests.

If the gathering is of twenty or more people, leave every member of your organisation the empowerment to order on behalf of the client, if s/he demands. If you are the senior most, it is your duty to tell everyone in advance.

If you are a client, then sit back and enjoy all courtesies offered. Use the word 'prefer' rather than 'want', in case you want to order anything. You can always show off your art of cutlery and chopsticks, etc. You may use your fingers to eat if your culture allows it, but do keep the ambience in mind and the place you are at. We have covered eating with hands in another session. Do read that through.

Do not make use of cutlery, if you feel your client might feel uncomfortable with it. Even if you are good at eating with chopsticks, avoid eating with them if your client does not ask for it. Your focus should be more on the client rather than on the food and drinks.

If you are invited, you do not have to show your courtesies for the bill. The host pays. If you are the host, it looks good when you have already submitted your credit card with the cashier and they just debit it from your card and come to you for your signature. Tipping is very important, even if it is a buffet meal. Without the waiters clearing out your tables and getting you your drinks, your meal would not have been so enjoyable.

Making chewing noises, touching food with your hand, using a toothpick without covering your mouth with your hand, burping out loud, sneezing without covering your mouth with both hands and a tissue, scratching your head or coughing without covering your mouth may not go down too well with your hosts. If you have a runny nose, make sure you are using your personal handkerchief or carry a packet of tissues. Do not ever blow your nose in front of anyone sitting at the dinner table. If you cannot control it, make sure you go to the washroom and freshen yourself.

Dressing for both sides is formal attire, or at most semi-casual.

## Meal with your Boss or Senior

First of all congratulations to you, if you get invited home by your boss. You can be rest assured your boss values your association beyond business. Remember, s/he is compromising his/her holiday to organise a meal for you at home. So never miss an opportunity to attend such a gathering.

You must carry some souvenir with you. Avoid taking personal stuff for anyone at home. Take something like a pen for the boss, or something personal for the spouse, or toys for kids. Home appliances are not recommended. Buy something unique and valuable. You may also carry chocolates and candies for the kids.

The rest goes as per what has been mentioned above.

## Outing with Families and Office Colleagues

Dress up for your vacation, be trendy and comfortable. Make your plan according to your destination. Be participative while travelling, have complete fun whether you are a senior or a junior. Meet everyone with their family and introduce your family to everyone. Be with the group and do not act superior or inferior. Read up about the place you are visiting so that you may share those insights with all. Do read the session on 'Official Travelling' to give you more insight into this as well.

The more you keep involved in group activities, the better it is. Remember you are out to enjoy yourself. So make the most of it, without disturbing anyone.

If you are carrying a camera, make sure you click photographs of everyone around rather than just your family.

Do treat all kids as your own. Carry some common medicines for headaches, vomiting, temperature, stomach upsets, etc., with you. It might come in handy.

There are other occasions as well when people around you get to explore things, like unorganised drinks among friends, one on one dinner or lunch, etc. Be casual only if you are with trustworthy and close friends. If you know that you speak too much after drinks, avoid getting drunk unless you are with very close friends.

These are some moments when your colleagues get to see the other side of you rather than your professional side. But this is a test of a different nature. Opinions are made about you here as well, with your every gesture and your behaviour. People do keep in mind your image in office when they deal with you. This could be a good opportunity for you to convey that when you business, you mean business; and when you are out to have fun, you let your hair down, and you are ahead in both.

You are half done by now in building your brand with this session. But, there is yet another half to cover. You may feel by now, that it is so tough to be under a testing radar all the time. You may also be wondering if it is really possible for anyone to be this perfect on all the occasions that we have discussed till now. Building a brand seems to be more difficult than building performance purely based on work. You might think that you should focus on hard work and then get ahead in life rather than picking up these professional acting skills.

But the fact of the matter is that we have discussed what you have already been doing everyday in your office life, and what you have to do in addition, and there is no other way around it. The only thing we are adding to this overview is that we are making you conscious of what may be perceived as a desirable thing to do and what may be perceived as unfavourable. What people take notice of and what people usually ignore. And, we are working towards polishing and refining those skills. Don't you like polished and refined things more when you are out shopping? It's simple and practical. Isn't it?

There is another important situation all of us come across. This is especially relevant for people on field jobs and others who have climbed higher up the success ladder. Official travelling. Let's pack up for the day and learn some existing rules of official travelling.

should focus on hard work and then get ahead in life rather than picking up these professional acting skills.

But the fact of the matter is that we have discussed what you have already been doing every day in your office life and what you have to [illegible] addition, and there is no other way around it. The only thing we are adding to this overview is that we are making you conscious of what may be perceived as a desirable thing to do and what may be perceived as unfavourable. What people take notice of and what people usually ignore. And we are working towards polishing and refining these skills. Don't you like polished and refined things more when you are out shopping? It's simple and practical, isn't it?

There is another important situation [illegible] of us being actors. This is especially relevant for people on field jobs and others who have climbed higher up the success ladder. Official travelling. Let's pack up for the day and learn some existing rules of official travelling.

'When travelling for work, add some fun too, and when travelling for fun, *DO NOT* add work.'

# Session V

# TRAVEL

Most of us have to travel as part of our job profile, unless your job is sedentary. You need to be touring officially – be it for an 'incentive tour' that you might have won for hitting that jackpot target, or on official duty – making sure your marketplace is working the way you have designed it to work! Whatever the case may be, we urge you to keep certain details in mind, to be that colleague who is a pleasure to be with.

Whether you are travelling alone or with your colleagues and seniors, it is important for you to take note of the seemingly small but extremely impressionable gestures. Whether you are travelling by car, bus, train, or by air – right from booking a cab to waiting at the airport/bus stand/railway station for your colleague to arrive and sharing a room – every aspect needs to be meticulously planned and executed! Humans by nature are selfish. Most of us become selfish while travelling, whether it means grabbing the best seat or an empty seat in a crowded compartment or pushing each other while getting in, placing your luggage or standing in queue for tickets. We do not realise that such gestures are noticed and it immediately makes an impression about us. While travelling, you are still on show, so you must be at your best there too.

**Be on Time**

Make sure you plan well to be ON TIME. As it is said, you realise the importance of one minute when you are a minute late to catch your train. It doesn't help in any way to be late and keep your colleagues waiting for you. Punctuality as a virtue is most desired in this particular occasion. If by any chance you are running late, please call your senior (if s/he is travelling with you) and one other peer or junior, and have that person inform the rest that you called mentioning that you're running late. Otherwise you might leave your colleagues in an embarrassing situation. We remember one amusing incident that we would like to share with you. Two colleagues – Shweta and Sunil were travelling together. Sunil had already reached the airport and taken his boarding pass. He wanted to take the boarding pass for Shweta too, as she was already late; but it's compulsory for the person to be present there to get a boarding pass. A thought struck him, he went up to the counter and said, 'I would like the boarding pass for Shweta.' The counter staff refused, asked where the passenger was. He just gestured towards the seating area of the airport, and said, 'Do you expect Madam to come and get her boarding pass herself? (using a tone to indicate that she was too big to collect her boarding pass, like a celebrity, and that he was the assistant sent to collect the ticket on her behalf)'. Then he added, 'Please be quick, I have to fetch some coffee for her now!'. Not sure what the counter staff thought, he received the boarding pass. Had Sunil not taken her boarding pass she would have missed her flight! We're not saying that this is the best way to travel. In fact, it is imperative to be 'on time, everytime'. This was just one of those amusing incidents we wanted to share with you. It also shows that travelling with colleagues on work is not always boring!

**Seat Selection**

If you are travelling with your senior, take the opportunity to stand in queue for them. If you are taking tickets together, this means your senior is okay with you taking a seat next to him/her. Some people do prefer to sit alone as they enjoy taking a nap or reading. Some seniors might do it to keep a distance from juniors. The first preference for seats should be given to ladies. A lady colleague (senior or junior) should always be offered to be seated by the window or in the aisle. Her comfort should be thought about first. It works better to let her choose her seat! Even if your seat number is the one that she chooses to sit on, please do not mention it. That's the worst impression you could create. It's also not nice to already be seated in your designated seat just because you reached earlier, and not offer her a seating choice, when she arrives.

Window seats or aisle seats are the most preferred. If you're travelling with your senior and you have to make the choice of seating, please choose the middle seat.

### Luggage

Always keep good quality and clean luggage. Broken suitcases, obnoxious colours, non-branded bags are not recommended. Have an option for both small and big suitcase/bag. If you are travelling for a day, your luggage should not be too big.

Do not overdo your enthusiasm in helping seniors or ladies with their luggage, unless s/he is unwell or not able to do it. Be very careful while handling your luggage. Make sure you do not hit anyone. Do not mishandle other's luggage while placing yours; if you have to move somebody's luggage it is better to ask the person concerned.

### During Flight

Do not expect too many reminders from the air hostess to switch off your phone. It is not a matter to boast about, to use your phone without letting the air hostess know. You have to respect the safety of others. Do carry along some interesting reading material for yourself. If you are fond of sleeping, mind your sleeping posture, you should not be falling asleep on your neighbour's shoulders. If your seniors or colleagues want to sleep, do not initiate any conversation.

Do not stare at the air hostess or ladies sitting around you. Show your politeness and manners.

### Travelling in a Car

There are times when the journeys are short and using the office cab seems to be the best option. The first rule to follow is that the senior most people get picked up last, unless it is really out of the way to do so. Even if it is a bit out of the way and means taking a slight deviation, it's wise to pick the seniors last and drop them off first. The other option could be to meet up at the office and for everybody to assemble there.

The second thing to keep in mind is to carry a small snack in case you get hungry. The others might eat larger meals and can sustain themselves longer. Making the entire group (or even if it is just one other person besides you) wait while you grab a bite is not advisable. Carry water for sure!

The front seat is yours if you are travelling with two or more seniors, unless one of them wants to sit there. If there is just one other person, the senior sits on the left hand side and you sit alongside him/her on the right hand side. If it is a multi-utility vehicle (like an Innova) and the front seat is taken, you take the seat behind, or the last row, if there are seniors travelling with you.

These are not things that demarcate status. The corporate world today is not so formal. But then there are these few things that if you keep in mind, will make you a desirable employee. A little bit of discomfort here and there pays in the long run. These are just gestures that make you a more likeable and endearing person, and let us tell you that it helps!

Here, since it would be a smaller group, apart from discussing work (which is unavoidable), it's desirable to discuss current affairs, business trends and your take on things that matter to the country's overall growth, etc. This is better appreciated than jokes and songs.

## Hotel Stay

Take the lead in completing check-in formalities for your seniors. Organising the best rooms for your seniors or bosses is always a good idea. Anyone would prefer to be given the best amenities within the company's budget. Book the best hotel as per the limit, do not compromise on a comfortable stay. If you have been given the responsibility to book the hotel, you will be held responsible if anything goes wrong.

It is always good to have a helpful attitude; it always helps if by nature you are willing to serve. Once you have this trait, it would come naturally to you to help and take care of small things which would help build your impression. If you are showing around colleagues who are visiting your city, make sure you know your city well – popular roadside eating joints and restaurants, the specialty of the place, traditional and ethnic shopping arcades, good and decent pubs and bars, etc. You should know historical facts and the unique aspects of the city to talk about, and recommend to visitors. Empower them with tips on how to manage around the city in case you are not accompanying them. You must however, make it a point to offer to accompany them.

Your instructions to the hotel staff about the billing should be clear – whether the visitor will pay directly or if the bill is to be presented or not. If your seniors are visiting a small town, do make arrangements for newspapers, amenities in the room and bathroom, etc. It is always better to inform everyone in advance about amenities available in the hotel. Some people might like to come prepared in terms of getting their gym kit, swimsuits, shorts, etc.

## Sharing a Room

There are times, especially as a junior in the corporate world, when you are expected to share a room with a colleague.

There are some details that we urge you never to overlook. Sharing space for some may be the most difficult thing to do, while for others it may be quite comfortable. So, it is always better to keep in mind the colleague who is uncomfortable, so that all grounds are covered. Your behaviour during 'space sharing' makes a very impressionable statement about you as a person and a colleague. Let me (Mamata) give you an instance from my life, about how an impression can be made from the way you share space. I remember this one time I was expected to share space and I was waiting for the rooming list, anxious beyond words to know who I would have to put up with (I am very finicky in my habits and hygiene is very high on my agenda). Finally the long dreaded list arrived in my inbox. I now knew who 'that' person was. I wasn't particularly close to this colleague and hadn't spoken much with her till then. In fact, I felt she was 'not my type' – whatever that means! But then I am a very positive person, so I took this challenge and charged right ahead. I would overcome whatever came my way.

Today all I can say is that whenever I am required to share a room for an official tour, we manipulate the rooming list (much to the organisers' disappointment) just to be able to be together. I love my stay with her. In fact, I look forward to it as we have now become good friends and we can do a lot of catching up with our after-dinner chats when we retire for the night. How does this beautiful impression get built? You will get to know as you read this session. Much of what is in it is inspired by her!

When you are sharing a room with a colleague keep in mind the following points:

**Bedroom manners:** Keeping every small thing in its designated space is the key. Keep your clothes neatly packed inside your suitcase or fold them neatly in a pile and put it away in an almirah/wardrobe. Keep your shoes neatly tucked away in a corner so it doesn't come in the way of your roommate. Socks should be kept right on top of your shoes, not lying around here and there. Should you want to use the free space available to both of you, you should mention it by saying, 'Hey I'm putting my keys, phone, perfume, etc., here.' It's not taking permission; it's just respecting the other person's right to that space as well. If the almirahs are not separate, follow the same rule. Just remember to mention it.

Don't keep the light on till odd hours of the night, even if it is the light towards your side of the room. If it disturbs the other person even remotely, you should be extra careful. If you want to read or do something else till late, mention it to your roommate and keep only the reading light on.

Ask before putting the TV on. 'I think I'll watch TV for sometime' is an acceptable statement. Keep the volume at acceptable levels. If it is possible, you may switch to a channel that's of common interest to both of you. That way you will also build a bond with each other. If s/he doesn't want to watch TV with you, ensure that the volume is at an acceptable level.

**Ordering room service:** Please do not order room service only for yourself. I have an example to share here. We had gone to

Goa on an official trip. I was sharing a room with a colleague. I went for a shower, only to return to the bedroom to find her gorging on a jumbo-size sandwich. She had ordered room service. I was shocked. Then she opened a packet of cashewnuts, offered it to me, I declined; she then put on the TV, and started munching on cashews while watching TV.

Then there will be stuff in the mini fridge that you need to pay for. Before popping open a bottle from there, please mention to your roommate that you are aware it's chargeable and that you are okay with it. Please do offer the beverage to your roommate. Just because you will pay for it, it isn't okay for you not to offer it to him/her.

**Using the hotel phone:** The same rule applies as in popping chargeable bottles from the hotel mini fridge.

Should you want to venture out of the room, do let your roommate know you'll be out for a while. Don't just disappear and reappear after an hour. S/he might have plans and don't forget – you share the key to your room. If you're out with friends and have gotten delayed, make it a point to call your roommate. Ask what would be the best way you can sneak into the room without disturbing him/her. And, before bringing a friend into the room, you must ask permission. You must not say – 'Hey I've got a friend with me' or 'Meet my friend so and so'. It would be better to say 'Do you mind if I bring along a friend to our room this evening?' It's actually 'taking permission', not 'merely informing'!

**Avoid borrowing:** Take permission before borrowing ANYTHING ... anything at all, however insignificant. The best rule is to avoid borrowing unless it's absolutely necessary.

**Bathroom manners**: Please bring along ALL the toiletries that you require. Borrowing toiletries is simply not acceptable. Keep them all on one side of the bathroom without cluttering the entire shelf.

Once you have finished using the bathroom, leave it in the cleanest possible manner, and keep it as dry as possible. Wipe off all the water from the basin plank. Put the used towels in the laundry bag or basket. If you're using your own towel, find a place to dry it, in the balcony or someplace like that. Wipe off the seat of the toilet if it is wet.

If you are visiting a friend (however close) or colleague in his/her hotel room, please do ask for permission before you use the bathroom. Gesturing towards the bathroom and saying 'May I?' is good enough. Ask permission before using anything – even a tissue!

### A Small Tip

Carry a small gift if possible, for the person you are going to share the room with. Even something like the delicacy sweet of your region or any specialty, makes a lot of difference. Of course, it's not a must, it's just a value addition.

### Travelling by Train or Bus

If you are the first one to reach, please get into the train/bus, find your seats and make sure everything is all right. Should you need to buy some food and drinks for the journey, do so while you are waiting for your colleagues to arrive. Buy at least a little bit to suffice for a couple of people. It's very impolite to buy edibles only for yourself. If you are running on a tight personal budget, it makes sense to carry water from home and some homemade food (that works out much cheaper). But, never carry food and drinks only for yourself. Sometimes the journey may be long and you would have carried your favourite sweet that you don't normally like to share. But while travelling with colleagues please be sure to share. Do not take your food out at night, when everyone else is sleeping, and eat it alone.

When you order common food for all, which normally happens during long train journeys, please do not pounce on the food as soon as it arrives. Also, don't grab the best portions of the food and pile up your plate. Yes, we know it's difficult to resist good food, we are both foodies ourselves, but let us tell you dear reader, we've learnt from experience that it's better to let go of some good food, rather than letting go of that most coveted 'impression'.

Travelling with colleagues is such fun, if you are able to carry off your manners and etiquette, and be a pleasurable person to be around. Your manners and behaviour not only helps you climb the ladder, it also helps to get work done when you're back in office. You are accepted as a person who is so endearing that people would love to help you when you are stuck at work. On the other hand, if proper manners are not displayed at these times you are looked at as more of a pest the rest of the time! And being known as a pest isn't exactly how you would like to lead your life in office!

## Some Tips for Train and Bus Journeys

Carry some jokes, some real-life amusing incidents, memories of some popular songs, and be abreast of the latest hot topics surrounding our country's affairs or our popular celebrities. You'll make quite an impression by dishing them out. But then again, you have to apply caution and make sure that you don't overdo it. Give everyone a chance to relate their own jokes and stories, and you may speak about your own only when you find a gap! Striking a balance is the key here too, like in all other situations.

Carry some homemade food or some specialty of your region and share freely with all.

Join the group in whatever they wish to do. Don't be stuck to your I-pod or phone when the rest are playing 'Antakshri'. Even if you do not understand the game or the songs, join the fun. Fun we all understand, don't we? We've found it always works better when you blend in instead of sticking out like a sore thumb!

Be honest in submitting your travel bills. All companies do not expect you to make money out of travelling. You are recommended to strike off items which are not to be claimed as per company policy. No organisation accepts liquor and cigarette bills. Good organisations do not want employees to spend their money on basic requirements. In some ways, HR policies do cover tips and non-bill items for compensation. Making a small amount of money through artificial bills is not recommended at all, this small amount will cost you millions of rupees worth of impression. Sometime it may happen that you lose your brand value for life. Be on time in submitting your claims.

The days have been tiring and the market visit is successful. After reaching home late at night you just have enough time for a good sleep and must hit office the next morning. The day is Friday, after half a day the entire office will bear a weekend mood, most of your close ones and direct reportees will come and see you. You will have a lot of time for yourself and to catch up with other colleagues across corridors and corners. And that brings to you yet another opportunity to show performance and build your brand.

"There is always a foolish corner in the wisest organisation. Corridors are like roads for fire brigades and ambulances because that's where all the fireworks and accidents happen in office."

# Session VI

**Do not slouch** – [illegible] indifference and [illegible] affect your [illegible] posture [illegible] attitude.

**Do not stray off your seat** [illegible]

**Hands** – Don't play [illegible]

[illegible] Don't [illegible] around your hands too much [illegible] clasped, and [illegible] This is by far the most [illegible] be used with a colleague. Pointing fingers [illegible] is not acceptable at all.

**Legs** – Crossed legs look very elegant and confident. If you are not in the habit of crossing your legs then just keep them parallel together. Do not squeeze them [illegible] each other or [illegible] open them wide apart.

**Smile** – Last but not the least is this [illegible] called the SMILE. [illegible] qualities [illegible] brings a sense of warmth to all involved in the [illegible]. This is one gesture that can make or break your conversation. It's "oh so" important.

So much about body language. This should be enough to get you going. Let's get on to the other important [illegible] of spoken communication.

When you are in the middle of a [illegible] a pause and then react – you need not react immediately. It seems to the other person that you are in control, calm and composed, and you are also taken more seriously. You definitely

# OFFICE CORRIDORS AND CORNERS

Office corridors and corners are those places that are of the highest significance while building your professional personality and displaying your fine corporate etiquette, creating a good impression and building a desirable brand. Your office colleagues who are not directly related to your work only meet you in office corridors, the cafeteria, tea stalls, common recreational rooms or smoking zones. This is one situation where we speak casually, and most of the time on non-official topics. This is one spot where we get to update ourselves with the latest news within or outside office, gossip, affairs, figures or planning for weekend or evening outings, etc. In this session we will cover all situations other than your spending time in meetings, mails, etc.

What is the first spot you hit the when you start your day in office? Vehicle Parking!

## Parking

Parking space has become a big issue in almost every city in India. So, utter sensitivity is required in this area. Most organisations make extra efforts to ensure convenient parking for their employees. Vehicles parked safely and securely allow employees to concentrate on work.

Please ensure you follow the parking area rules before you enter the parking zone. Speed limit, no-honking, driving in arrow-marked lanes, are some of the critical rules to be followed. You must always stick to your space, and if someone else has accidentally parked in your designated space, please sort it out with the facilities department and do not park your car/ bike elsewhere. Picking up a fight with the security personnel is totally unacceptable. While parking, please ensure you park in the area that has been demarcated, making it easier for the person parking on either side, or front and behind.

If you happen to arrive at the parking area together with your seniors or boss, allow them to park their car first and follow them after they have parked. Similarly, while exiting in a similar situation, allow your seniors to exit first and follow later.

## Lift Manners

The lift is one area where you stand closer to people than in normal circumstances. This demands optimal use of space for some time.

When you have noticed that a colleague of yours is also parking at the same time as you, it is advisable to wait for him/her and proceed to the lift together. Holding the lift for a few seconds for your colleague to run in, is quite acceptable and in fact, welcome.

But then, holding the lift for more than a few seconds is just not acceptable. Everyone is in a hurry in the morning to show up at their workplace as early as possible. Someone might have a very important meeting to attend. Holding up the lift is a very sensitive issue and to be used with much caution. While in the lift, just a smile or a nod to everyone you can recognise is indeed a very pleasing attribute. You need not show overt signs of greeting, just a nod or a smile is enough. Remember, a lift is a very small area, so everything you do there is magnified. Talking on the phone could be quite disturbing to your fellow passengers, which of course you cannot help sometimes because you may be on an important call (pacifying your angry partner for not showing up last evening). But if you have to talk, keep the volume as low as possible. One blessing of the GSM mobile technology is that, more often than not, the cellphone stops working in a lift; so this point might not be so difficult to follow.

See that your laptop or your lunchbox is not banging against someone. Make sure you hold your laptop bag in your hand and do not use the sling option, so that you do not cover extra space.

Always let women, elders and children get into a lift first. Always keep note that nobody is within door closing range of a lift.

Be extra careful if there is a member of the opposite sex in the lift. See that you maintain a good and comfortable distance. For women, in a crowded lift, you may just carry your handbag or laptop bag in front, so as to avoid collision that makes you uncomfortable. Do not stand in a posture where your underarm is exposed; if you have bad body odour, please ensure decent deodorant. If you have to sneeze or cough, ensure minimal noise or action and definitely cover your mouth and nose while doing so.

If you are standing next to the door, ensure you give enough space for people to get out comfortably, even if it means you have to get out of the lift and get in again.

Do not stare at anyone, at any point of time, but especially in a lift. In that small space, any action seems magnified and hence uncomfortable.

When you want to go up in a lift, push only the up arrow button. Similarly when you want to go down, use the down arrow. Pushing both buttons is one of the most ignorant things you can do. And repeatedly pressing a button, whether up or down is also a sign of extreme ignorance. When there are others waiting with you, who you have noticed have pushed both buttons, there is no harm in indulging in this small gyaan giving session. It will save people from a lot of trouble in future. If you are next to the panel of buttons (not a very pleasant place to be), offer to press buttons for your lift mates.

### Holding the Door for your Colleague

While entering the office, hold the door for whosoever is behind you. Discriminating about that person being junior or senior in the organisation, and then deciding to hold the door should not occur to you at all. Even if it is the office boy/assistant, housekeeping staff, whoever the person is, they should be treated with respect. Here let us just make a brief mention –

in any situation in your work life, dignity of labour should be given foremost importance in your mind.

## Greeting your Colleagues

While entering the office you will again come across all your colleagues; here a nod or a smile or a soft good morning (good evening for some working in the night shift) is more than enough. You may also make a victory sign with your fingers, or a salute, or anything that suits your style. You can go on to make this your style statement in fact. Being loud and extra cheerful seems out of place. There's a term we would use for those colleagues of ours who would be extra loud and extra cheerful and pat most colleagues on their back early in the morning – 'enthu cutlet'!

Another thing to keep in mind is not to bring up anything about a mail that you might have sent to which you are expecting a response, or a report that you might be expecting from a colleague, when you meet that colleague first thing in the morning or evening – either at the parking lot, or lift, or just as you enter office. It's only fair to let everyone settle in and then approach them for something that is due from their side. This holds true even when you are leaving office and meet in the lift or any other place. And, of course, there is absolutely no need to specially go to your bosses' cabins to wish them. Wishing people as you meet along the corridors is good enough. Going to a person's cabin to wish them is really cheesy, but if you feel your boss expects it from you, go right ahead.

### Use your Coffee/Tea Time

You may go for a smoke or for coffee with your colleagues. That is the best time to discuss your worries over work, or something that has been due from that colleague, or some project that you might be working on together that needs extra attention. This is the perfect time to sort out all professional differences that you may have. It's casual and at the same time you get your message across. It's a nice way to tackle sensitive issues too, over laughter and jokes, but the message is sent across! If you happen to meet your boss in the smoking zone, it's nice to just pull your hand down (the one that is holding the cigarette), let him/her cross over and then start smoking. It's not like you are not supposed to smoke in front of your boss/seniors, but this is just a mark of respect that will leave a nice impression in the mind of the senior/boss. When there's a colleague of the opposite gender smoking, absolutely avoid giving comments or general gyaan on how smoking adversely affects his/her gender or our acceptance of smoking in Indian culture, etc. Just be cool and natural and behave normally like you would when smoking with a colleague of the same gender. Making someone uncomfortable is totally avoidable when we are trying to build a positive impression. You need to be cautious which side you are blowing your smoke, it is advisable to change your direction to the direction of the air. Make sure you keep the smoking area clean and ensure you throw the butts in the designated space.

While offering cigarettes to your colleagues, slide one cigarette out to offer so that it is easy for him/her to pick one. If you have to offer a light for a cigarette, always light from a distance and slowly bring it closer to the cigarette to avoid burning the person's hair or hand.

It is believed you are not supposed to light more than two cigarettes with one light, and many believe the following story. Once, an army officer was standing near the border line, at night, along with two colleagues. He lit a cigarette and then another and went on to light yet another. By the time he was to light the cigarette of the third officer, the enemy could spot them and he was shot. Ever since, it is believed that you do not light a cigarette for three people at the same time, as it is unlucky for the third person.

Whether you believe in this story or not (or many others like these), it is imperative to be sensitive towards the belief of others. There is no harm following some rituals that do not demand too much from you.

## Manage Your Time when the Server is Down

What do you do when your mail server is suddenly down. Like we have mentioned in our session 'communication', a major part of your day is spent on emails, so when the server is down, you feel lost. It's as if everything has come to a standstill. What do you do? Utilise this time to bond with your fellow colleagues and seniors. Share a joke or two. Discuss the current events which are interesting to most people. Or you may prepone some meeting that you had planned later in the day. This is also a good time to head out of office and meet a couple of customers and get real-time feedback from them about your products and services. This will be very well appreciated by all – peers and seniors alike.

**Handling the Restroom**

There are times you meet your colleagues in the restroom. Here again, major greetings are not required. A nod should do the job of a greeting. Of course, there is no need to be out of place when you bump into your boss in the restroom. It's natural – everybody needs to use the restroom. This reminds us of a boss that we had. Invariably, one of our teammates would meet our boss in the loo and this boss had the habit of asking '*Kya ho rahan hai?* (what's happening?)' and he would look insistently at this teammate, expecting an answer from him. Can you imagine this situation? How would you answer? Our teammate was always tempted to say, '*Yahan aur kya ho sakta hai boss?* (What else can be happening here boss?)' And then if there was no answer from the other person, the boss would ask about some data that he had presented, or some report that he ought to have sent, or ask about the intensity of sales action that is happening in the field, etc. We would often hear this story and we still always have a hearty laugh over it.

Once you are done using the restroom, please make sure you wash your hands. This example reminds us of another boss who apparently would just wet his fingers with the water trickling down from the water sink kept to flush out the toilet. They may not be aware of it, but they are the laughing stock over smoke breaks and coffee breaks. Would you like to be one of those people that others make a joke out of? Definitely not. That is why you are reading this book. So, this is the right time for you to learn about some of the desirable qualities of a civilised corporate citizen.

## Gossiping

This is one of the favourite pastimes of human beings, both male or female, be it in the gym, at home or in the workplace. It may be a good pastime at home where you are among family and friends who mean well; in the workplace, however, it may not be the ideal thing to do. At least not till you have gathered enough close colleagues who you can trust. What sometimes happens is that your talks are used against you and that may land you in unnecessary trouble. It is best to stay away from gossip. If you just cannot resist it, share it with colleagues who you know won't use it against you at any point of time. If you don't have any such colleague, it is definitely better to hold back – practise refrain. You would come across many characters in the workplace and they would enjoy dealing in double-talk. This sort of thing happens a lot in the corporate world, and you can never master this art, let us tell you. And if you cannot master an art, don't indulge in it. Stay away from gossip!

## Exit Time

This is the best time of the day for most of us. We may have family back home who we love to spend the evening with. However, there may be people whose families live away and so may prefer to hang around in office. Don't get caught in this situation ever. If you have completed your work for the day, please leave. You don't have to worry about whether your boss has left or not. Once you are done with your work, just inform your boss and leave. The sooner you understand this, the better. If you get caught into staying back late in office, this might develop into a habit and that is detrimental to the happiness and health of your family. Every person needs a balance in life. If you have a healthy life otherwise, you will perform better in office too. We have a friend who lives in Copenhagen. He mentioned that his company was demanding a four day week. They have to complete forty hours of work a week, which they claim they would do it in four days. We wonder if they succeeded, but what we are trying to say is that you must maintain a balance between home and office. Develop other interests, like painting or photography or playing a musical instrument, if there is nothing to look forward to at home, and if your family is away.

When you're leaving and you see a colleague waiting for public transport, if you have a vehicle, always ask if s/he is going in the same direction and offer a lift up to a common point. You must never ignore a colleague.

These are some of the things that you do apart from reading and replying to mails, apart from attending or conducting meetings, apart from attending to or making business calls, etc. These are the times your true nature unfolds and hence the right time to make the correct impression.

## SOME INTERPERSONAL EQUATIONS

We often find that when the word 'interpersonal' is used in an office environment – anywhere in the corporate world, we normally hear things like 'Teamwork' – 'How to motivate your team', 'How to be a good listener', 'Delegation and leadership skills', etc.

'Always smile', 'Be positive', 'Don't criticise' – are the recommendations that are usually offered. We do not refute that these are indeed required, during reviews, meetings, working with your team and other such professional set-ups. There are many institutions offering training programmes to address these. However, there are some very sensitive interpersonal equations one needs to deal with along the office 'corridors and corners', especially while dealing with colleagues on a day-to-day basis, and those are what we wish to address here.

### Dealing with a Girlfriend/Boyfriend in the Same Office

This happens very often. We could have just said – avoid it. Yes that's the best way no doubt, but how do you avoid matters of the heart? You spend a good part of your life in office, so this is bound to happen. However, there are some simple rules of conduct one ought to keep in mind while pursuing a romantic relationship at one's workplace. The first thing to remember is that once in office you are colleagues like any other. If you just keep this simple fact in mind, you will avoid all kinds of disaster that are normally seen in these situations. Treat your partner as any other colleague. When we say 'treat' we mean the way you look at each other, the way you talk, share a coffee, go through a presentation, etc., shouldn't be any different from what you do with the others. If you can follow the second rule, there's nothing like it. This is a sure shot success. Keep your relationship a secret till you are ready to make a long-term commitment, as in till you actually invite your colleagues to your wedding. And, its possible. We have seen it happen many times. Besides anything else, it will save you a lot of hassle. It's a human tendency to start looking at people in a relationship differently as soon as you find out about a close relationship.

Even if you make every attempt to treat each other like any other colleague in office, people will not let you be. They will find a difference in treatment even if there is none. All your colleagues are not from similar backgrounds or do not have a similar mentality. Many colleagues will not refrain from teasing you both, or passing undesirable comments. Talking behind your back happens often. So, if you can, please keep it a secret till you are able to.

But if the word is out already, these are some precautions you may take. Like the first thing we mentioned, treat each other as any other colleague. Do not give much heed to what people are talking about. Don't let it affect your relationship. Avoid sticking to each other at every coffee break or lunch break. Avoid working together late into the night. Avoid talking about your weekend adventures. If you really want to share your adventures, do it with friends outside office.

### Dealing with Irritable Characters

Indeed all kinds of people make the world. So, it is inevitable that you will come across people who irritate you. Some are pests, some are gossipmongers, some are chronic complainers, some are backbiters and some are overfriendly. Dealing with people who you don't like or who irritate you is a tough deal, especially if that person happens to be your boss! Just imagine a boss you cannot stand as a person! Tough indeed! However, just like you cannot choose your family, so also you cannot choose the colleagues you have to work with. So how do you handle these people while keeping your sanity intact? While dealing with peers and junior colleagues one simple rule applies – IGNORE

THEM. Be polite to them if you are face-to-face, but ignore what they are saying or doing or if they are trying to impress you (in these situations a fake smile works – they will see through it, hopefully). 'Ignore' definitely doesn't mean to be rude or impolite. There is a skill in ignoring people politely. Master that skill. It cannot be written down in words here, else we would have done so. But, imagine if that person is your boss or an influential senior member. Yes life could be that painful; you might actually land up with a boss that you cannot get along with at all. What do you do then? Just accept your fate and move on? Not really. You can deal with the bosses too. If you are having trouble with your boss, the best thing is to have a face-to-face meeting with him/her. Mention all the things that are troubling you, politely but firmly. Mention instances when you had trouble with the way your boss behaved. It helps. At the end of the day, there is one thing you must realise. The irritating colleague should not affect you personally.

## Religious Ceremonies in Office

Living and working in India, you are bound to come across many religious ceremonies that are performed in office. You might not believe in them, but always remember there are an equal or larger number of people who do. So, respecting each other's religion, and religious beliefs and rituals is absolutely mandatory. You may not have any belief in rituals, you have the right to your opinion; however don't express your opinion in public, even to a set of close colleagues. Keep it to yourself. You may not want to attend certain ceremonies. Please don't force yourself. But, don't make a drama out of it. Avoid it discreetly.

Make an excuse – say you have to meet a client, or make a market visit, or have to leave early that day; and then leave. But never mention that you do not want to attend a certain religious function held in office because you don't believe in it. This is a very sensitive issue and should be dealt with with care and caution.

**Dealing with Gay/Lesbian Colleagues**

Please remember that being gay is natural; nobody is gay or lesbian by choice. Please do not laugh or pass remarks on gay or lesbian colleagues, not even behind their back. If you are dealing with gay/lesbian clients, you are not expected to change your behaviour towards them. Just be natural, the way you remain with other colleagues. Especially with the background most of us are brought up in, there is a learning curve indeed to deal with these sensitive matters. This you will learn along the way, much more than we can actually tell you here.

**Differently-Abled Colleagues**

Again, differently-abled people believe they are differently-abled. Just because a differently-abled person may not able to see/talk/walk, it doesn't mean that s/he is less intelligent, or has lesser calibre. In fact, differently-abled persons wish to be treated as equals, as they should be. There is absolutely no need to be extra kind or 'do' things for them. Be kind, as you are generally with everybody else. Never entertain the thought that s/he is different from you, especially in professional dealings.

## Sharing Common Space with one or more Colleagues

There are times when you may be required to share work space with a colleague. Especially at a time like this when real estate rates are at its peak, organisations expect people to share space. It could be a room when you are travelling together or even desk space, if there is a scarcity of space in the office. There are some basics that you must always keep in mind. Never litter the space. By now, you would have gathered how these basic things can and will impact the impression you are trying to build, or the way you will be looked upon as a person. We will cover sharing desk space here, and you will find sharing room space in the session on official travelling.

While you are sharing desk space, make sure you leave enough room for your colleague to keep his/her belongings. When you are conversing with someone on the phone, try to keep your volume as minimal as possible. Do not disturb your colleague every now and then, by conveying something that just crossed your mind, or to share a mail/SMS that triggered a thought. Ideally you should keep such conversations to about 10 per cent of the time you are working at your desk together. You may forward mails and SMSes as you would to a colleague seated further away. This s/he may read at his/her convenience. It's better to stop your urge to whine and complain, even if you have someone sitting right there who has no choice but to listen to you. We have found, more often than not, that it is just a passing phase and you will yourself get over it very soon. However, your colleague would be left with that lingering thought concerning you. The idea is to treat your colleague at your desk like you would have treated any other colleague sitting further away from you. Lest you come to be known as a pest!

### Getting too Curious about Personal Lives of Others

First of all, let's ask ourselves why someone else's life interests us so much? We have been looking for an answer for this for quite a while now and have found answers – however lopsided! First, we love to compare. Second, when we know of pain that someone else is going through, our pain seems lesser. Third, when we know of the story of others, we feel secure that we are not alone facing the drudgeries of life. Fourth, it makes for a good topic of conversation when we meet our other friends, outside of work. We can be the centre of attention for a while at least.

Now, that didn't sound too good, did it? But the truth is, whatever the reasons that make us interested in other people's personal lives, they are there in the subconscious. You may think you are interested only because people care and because you would like to help if you can. Agreed, all of that is true, we are not ruling that out. But, somewhere in the depths of our minds, if we care to dig deep down, we will see that the reasons mentioned by us are not totally untrue. Anyway, the whole idea of mentioning it was to let you know that it is rather unkind to be too curious about someone else's personal life. If a colleague proactively wants to share something with you and thinks you can add value, by all means go along with it. Listen carefully to every word that is being spoken. It's being told to you because your colleague thinks there's some value in speaking to you or maybe just to release frustration/excitement or s/he thinks you will add value with your suggestions. But, the key is to hear him/her completely without interfering with your own thoughts in between (there'll be enough time for you to do that). Listen with an open mind. Once they are through with all that they had to say, if any advice or suggestion has been sought from you, you may softly make your suggestion. If you get an affirmative answer, put across your own views on the situation very mildly. And do not expect that your advice will be followed just because you have been a confidante and your suggestions have been sought. We have found, more often than not, a person wants a listening ear, not a curious mind.

### Delighting your Colleagues

This doesn't take much effort. Just a wish on a birthday/anniversary. A simple SMS brings a smile to your colleagues' face. Wouldn't you want to do it? If you notice something different in your colleague's demeanour, just ask if everything is all right. If you notice that a colleague is looking extra fresh and happy one day, ask what the cause of their happiness is. They might not share if it's something very personal, but would appreciate the fact that you care, and that you notice. We are all human at the end of the day, corporate or otherwise. Human feelings and tendencies do not die down completely just because you are in a corporate atmosphere. Yes, it may be a little different and a bit more formal, but a smile is a smile, no matter where you are or what you do!!

### Visiting Hospitals and Funerals

As soon as you get news of someone being unwell, maybe even a distant colleague or a colleague you don't normally spend your leisure time with, make sure you send in an SMS with a 'get well soon' message. It will cost you only an SMS and a few seconds of your time, but the impression that you will leave in that person's mind will be long lasting. A person is at his/her weakest moment when one is unwell, so all well-wishers at this weak moment seem like a boon. Imagine yourself in the receiver's position and you will know what we mean. If you come to know that your colleague's close family hasn't been well, do enquire after him/her. If someone is in the hospital, an attempt to visit them in the hospital once is definitely desirable. So also for funerals. A call to your colleague if s/he has lost a loved one (God forbid!) is something you definitely shouldn't miss. But, try your level best to make it to the funeral as well. Offer to help with whatever you can, with the arrangements for the funeral, picking up and dropping relatives; just being by the side of the most impacted member. Just offer help! These are some values we have been brought up with since childhood, and we mustn't give them up no matter where we are, who the recipients are, whatever your position is vis-á-vis the effected person. This is the value system we must uphold with pride.

'Social networking is like knowledge; you can never say you are done with it.'

# Session VII

# SOCIAL NETWORKING

Almost everything we have shared till now is in a way about developing a social and professional circle of friends/colleagues/acquaintances. Hence, this is one topic that we cannot afford to overlook. It has crept into our lives in such a way that it has become a necessary evil. With the advent of technology and its continuous developing process at lightning speed, coupled with the current fast-moving lifestyle, neither you nor people around you have time for socialising. Weekdays have long working hours, and travelling to and fro takes your entire day and drains you of all your energy. This happens to the extent that the moment you get some time for yourself, you look forward to being alone and resting your mind to gain energy for the next working day. Whatever your opinion is, you cannot ignore the fact that technology has made life much easier today. Earlier you could meet or talk to only one person at a time and the time and effort required to do that was usually immense. Today, with the invention of SMS/social networking sites you are in touch with hundreds of friends and family members all the time, and, with minimal cost.

With all these developments, socialising has also developed with time. Celebrities talk to thousands of their fans at one point on a site like Twitter; you are able to share your photos, videos and experiences at the click of a button on social sites like Facebook and professional sites like LinkedIn. These sites were invented so as to help one develop friend circles and socialise, but it is catching up among professionals too. More importantly, employers and consultants are reviewing sites before recommending any candidate for new vacancies. It is but obvious that the way you present yourself on these sites will reflect your likes and dislikes and your style. You not only attract friends but also employers.

In this session we will focus on how you should build and maintain your network with friends, relatives, and colleagues. In your busy life, you can still maintain your social life and not allow people to complain about your absence.

As we discussed earlier, word of mouth plays an important role in your growth. When you remain in touch with your circle of influence consistently, with good intentions, you will generally be spoken about well in all circles. People attach value to the words spoken by your colleagues about you. You should leaving a good impression in every aspect that we have shared in all the previous sessions. Through networking you are only reinforcing it.

Networking has its own management, and with this aspect planned well you can get full marks in your socialising skills.

Do you think everyone around you expects to be in touch with you every day or week or month? Not everyone does and neither do they have the time.

Let's do some simple planning for your networking; once it is planned it is easy for you to keep a check on who you might have missed during socialising. You can create a table with columns for keeping in touch via 'SMS/chat', 'Phone call', 'Email/video conference' and 'Visit'. For better detail, add columns for birthdays/anniversaries and social networking sites like Facebook, Twitter and LinkedIn. Just fill in the names of the people you need to be in touch with and tick it in the box, under the categories of the way you need to be in touch with them.

Use other devices like your mobile and your laptop to remind you of important dates.

Once you are ready, you need to review this chart once a month and then use your mobile reminders accordingly. And, be updated in your social networking. Do not forget to update any names you happen to recall later!

Use the task or calendar application on your outlook email to keep a tab on important dates. If you are not sure what to say when you call, here are some tips:

- Give updates on all the latest developments on your side.
- Speak about any recent development on the other person's side.
- You can always call to take advice and guidance.
- Birthdays and anniversaries/promotions are good occasions to wish the person.

You have to socialise and you have to gain leverage on any opportunity to talk/call/visit. You need to ensure that your socialising is consistent. Maintaining consistency will surely lead to good word of mouth in times to come.

**Networking Profiles**

If you think that Facebook/LinkedIn/Twitter are only socialising sites, you will be surprised to hear that a lot of companies are looking at the facebook profiles of people they want to hire. And, if you have been cribbing about your company amongst your friend circle through these sites, it will have a negative affect. These sites are not casual anymore but extremely easy and a fast tool to be in touch with friends. Your profile is your character and it has to reflect who you are.

Social networking profiles are profiles without any question mark. Most people would like to know about you, your full name, where you're from, educational background, age, sex, marital status, where you are located currently, what are your professional and your personal interests, etc.

Your picture cannot be left blank for sure, and only upload your latest photo. It is recommended that you should be better looking in the photo than you actually are. A lot of people make the mistake of pasting a full-length photo as their profile picture. Your profile picture should have your face up close as it is much easier for anyone to identify on a small screen like a cellphone screen.

Your profile should be fun and confident.

Do not write what you are not.

You should not hesitate to join such sites; indeed it only helps you make new friends and allows you to be aware of the latest happenings in your friends' lives.

Avoid adding too many friends as it is not meant to be a number that you can boast about, it is indeed for your friends, who you would like to be in touch with. Do not allow people to add you unless they know you.

Being too active or too passive on such sites does not reflect well. Maintain a balance. Be selective in your comments.

‘An uncluttered desk reflects an uncluttered mind ... it helps you concentrate on the more impacting things in life.’

# Session VIII

# WORKSTATION

While we are on our journey to building a brand to reckon with, would you imagine, even the way you maintain your workstations/cabins, and how sensitive you are to your neighbouring workstations, says volumes about you.

These are some things we tend to ignore in the hectic schedule of the day. But, let us assure you, by managing your workstation/cabin well, you will definitely gain popularity among peers and seniors alike. You will be seen as a person who is easily accessible and quite sensitive to detailing. 'A keen eye for detail' is one of the most sought after attributes that an employer looks for.

### Clean Workstation

Needless to say, your workstation should be neat and tidy. However, it shouldn't be so neat that it looks clinical. It shouldn't seem like you spend more time in tidying up your workstation, rather than getting on with your work. Just ensure that the papers on your desk are not strewn around. Just stack them up. Your diary could be lying here and there on your desk somewhere and your pen can also be just lying around, not necessarily in the penstand. However, your marker pen, scissors, ruler, etc., should be inside the stand, as you do not need to use them all the time. Everything on your table should actually have their place. During the day or while working, it could be lying here and there, but at the end of the day or whenever you are free place them back in their spots. You might be wrong in thinking that rough paper stacking and things being scattered around gives the impression that you are hard-working. Managing your seat is a reflection of how you manage your work.

**Drawers**

One of the most important and difficult things to manage other than your desk are your drawers. Most people find themselves lazy when it comes to managing their drawers and they take advantage of drawers always remaining closed. It is always suggested to create blocks within drawers so that things kept in them do not move much while closing and opening the drawer. It takes just a few minutes of your time to discipline your drawer and to set a designated place for all the things you want to keep in the drawer. After that, you need to discipline yourself and keep ten minutes for your drawers once a week just to maintain that neatness. If you follow the discipline of placing things in their designated place right after use, you will not need to spend any time at all in maintaining a neat and tidy drawer.

## Papers

The second thing you need to manage are the papers on your table, which could be as per your role. Some papers you need to store with you for references or some that come through to your table for your intervention. In both scenarios, if you have an identified place for papers for filing and action required, like a folder, paper basket, etc., just keep them there.

## Photos

Make your workplace interesting for you, you will be spending at least one-third of your day at your seat. It should have an atmosphere that gives you a happy and beautiful feeling. Do manage some photographs of your best friend or your family. Make sure there are not too many. The photographs need not be overtly formal, but avoid photographs of you and your best friend saying cheers in a pub, holding two mugs of beer; or you and your partner cuddling up to each other. Basically, there are some things about your life best kept at home. The photos that you choose to keep at your office desk could be of a vacation in a scenic location, where you have posed formally for it. Or of your child/niece/nephew flashing a smile or your parents smiling at you. A photograph or two definitely adds value to your workstation; not only aesthetically but it also relieves you of your stress at work, when you just get a glimpse of your beautiful world back home. It reinforces the fact that this is after all only a job, so there is no point taking too much stress and tension at work. Whenever you are having too much trouble at work, just look at those photos at your desk and tell yourself that you are working to give the people in it a better life; and you will feel a renewed energy to face all odds, because you are taking the stress of a high-pressure job, only to give your loved ones a better life. This is what a simple photograph can do for you!

**Water Bottle**

Normally all offices have water bottles kept at each person's desk. You can be different. Get yourself a sleek water jug or a good-looking bottle. Get a smart glass as well. As much as possible, try and pour water into a glass and drink. Avoid drinking straight out of the bottle. You will be recognised as a person who does not accept average things in life and you will be looked upon as someone who aims for better things. This means you will work harder and more efficiently to get what you want. You will also be seen as a person who gives a lot of attention to detail. Yes, even this helps. Little drops of water make an ocean. You might have heard this before. So, these are those little drops that will help build you up as a desirable corporate citizen.

We suggest you get yourself a funky mug as well. A funky mug if you are young, and a sleek formal one if you are older. While everyone else drinks from a paper cup or the regular insipid office cups, you can choose to give yourself a treat by drinking your coffee or tea from a mug of your choice. You not only get noticed, but it speaks about your personality, and it also feels good to drink from a nice mug. But, please don't make a big deal out of this. Just be casual about it.

### Books

It does not matter what size your workstation/cabin might be, please keep a couple of books in it. Books on management or self-help books (this one for example), or even slightly philosophical books or books related to your industry and profession are suggested. We advise you not to keep novels in office, or fictional books. Books that have been presented to you by your colleagues or bosses are even better. Have them write a couple of lines on the first page. And, if you have any greeting cards given by your ex-colleagues during your farewell, you may display that for a couple of months when you join your new company.

### Whiteboard

A small board on your table is important for discussion and to jot down action items. Maintain your board regularly. If you have nothing to follow, keep it clean. It is a sign of efficiency.

### Pen Stand

The pen stand, paper case, visiting cards stand, etc., could all be handpicked by you on your travels. Or just go into a store and pick up what you like.

**Diary**

Your diary or notepad should be well-written and should show the seriousness of points mentioned for action. Signs like a tick mark, cross, circle or other important signs are good examples of making the best use of your diary/notepad. Try and make the best use of your diary calendar for meetings, calls, follow-ups, etc. It helps to improve your efficiency. Just imagine if someone follows up with you on a time decided by you and you do not remember it. You must update yourself.

**Eatables**

You must keep something in your drawers to munch on or for evening snacks. Chocolates, candies, some healthy fat-free or cholesterol free snack, even instant snacks like noodles, etc., are advisable if you have a microwave in your office. Generally, during late evening, most organisations serve evening snacks as you feel like munching on or eating something, especially if you sit late in office. This will really attract people to come to you and you will be easily differentiated among others. Moreover, every time you are host, you take the credit for it.

**Leaving for the Day**

As you leave for the day, your table should look clean and even your chair or any furniture should be placed properly. You would have noticed yourself getting upset about untidy or scattered cubicles and desks. How would you like to see your workstation when you come in to work next morning?

So you should place everything well before you leave and do not depend on housekeeping to do it for you.

## Some Tips

Keeping a small plant, your favourite or kid's favourite soft toy, winning trophies, unique table calendar, idols of god, etc., could also be handpicked by you to keep at your desk. This makes your workstation not only different and bright, but also makes your workstation very personal.

Do not sit with your shoes or sandals open as a habit, unless you have a temporary medical problem. If your cubicle has other workstations as well, mind your words and volume when you take phone calls. Just ensure that you are not disturbing others. Do not fall back on your chair in a sitting posture. Ensure that your colleagues do not come by too often to kill their time, and disturb you and your neighbours. You have to learn the art of saying 'no' and give a signal to avoid them.

It is not the only thing of course, but your workstation is an enhancer. Visual impacts stay longer in people's minds. Like other people, such things click with the boss as well. You may not be sure how often your boss comes to your desk, but surely you would go to your boss quite often and have the opportunity of noticing how s/he manages his/her cabin or cubicle or workstation, and then you will get a feel of his/her likings and nature.

## Rest of the Office

Do not litter your office. Absolutely avoid throwing stuff on the floor, even if you know for sure that no one is watching you. It should become your very nature to keep your office premises clean. Just because a portion of the office is not your work area, it doesn't mean you will not care for it. The entire office is yours and hence to be treated with the utmost respect.

In the pantry after having a meal, ensure you leave the table and chair absolutely clean. How would you feel when you arrive at the pantry with your stomach growling and you find all the tables littered with other people's leftovers? That's the worst thing you can do, and that reflects your attitude and grooming. Do not leave used plates on the table, clear all the crumbs that have fallen on the table while eating, and carry the used tissues and dump it in the garbage bin. While eating non-vegetarian food or vegetables like drumsticks, never ever keep the bones or the drumsticks on the table while you are at your meal. Ask for a side plate if that's available in your office pantry, or simply use the cover of your lunchbox to store them while you finish the rest of your meal. When you are eating non-vegetarian food alongside a vegetarian, be extra cautious and careful about the bones, if any. For vegetarians, leftover pieces of bones may be a very gory sight and they might even lose their appetite if they find them kept alongside their plates while they have their meal. Be sensitive and caring about other people's sentiments. That's the very basic of grooming and the foundation upon which to build a good impression.

Washroom behaviour is like footwear. You might have noticed people wearing expensive clothes and jewellery, but when your eyes lead you down to their feet it leaves you depressed. This normally happens because we feel that once we have worn good clothes and are looking reasonably good, no one notices our footwear. That is given the least importance. But actually, the reverse is true. Your footwear is a total giveaway of your basic hygiene and grooming. So also, in the washroom, even if no one can see you, you must ensure your best and cleanest behaviour while using it. Always flush well, and if the flush isn't working, don't just walk away. Please ensure the housekeeping staff fix it; only then are you ready to exit the washroom. Never be caught leaving the washroom without washing your hands. This is not only for others to see, but for your own benefit as well. You cannot imagine the number of bacteria that infest a washroom, no matter how clean it is kept. So wash your hands with soap, EVERYTIME. If you have the habit of combing your hair, ensure all fallen hair is gathered in a tissue and thrown in its rightful place, i.e., the garbage bin. If you have sprinkled water while using the wash basin, just take a tissue and give the area a quick swipe. If there are others waiting before you, wait for your turn and do not rush ahead. If it's an emergency, make it known to the people who are already waiting and then go ahead. Everybody understands how traumatic washroom emergencies can be. Hanging around in the washroom indulging in small talk is an absolute no-no.

The basic point to keep in mind is – Leave the washroom clean and dry after use.

With this we come to the end of this chapter, hoping we have been able to provide some amount of guidance on basic etiquette. The next session is an extra-sensitive session, as it deals with the most important person for you in your office. As there is management in everything, so there is management of the boss as well. Let's discuss by far the most sensitive and critical person – the boss – in the coming session.

"Boss is like a technology; if it works for you, it makes your life easier, if not ... even worse."

# Session IX

# BOSS

Boss is like a technology, if it works for you, it makes your life easier and if not, worse. Your immediate manager, supervisor, or senior in the corporate world practically decides your success and the pace of your career growth. As we have already discussed, you are a brand (this is the brand we have been helping you build from the first session onwards) and it is for sure that the co-author of building your brand name is your boss. In many of the human resources surveys on why people leave organisations, it has time and again been proven that people leave the organisation because of their bosses. It is said 'people leave their bosses, not the organisation'. But how many people join an organisation after being recommended by the boss, or who work under the same boss is not known. We are sure that percentile will be surprisingly high too.

Your boss is also human at the end of the day but as a professional s/he has to sometimes disguise him/herself as per his/her role. S/he might not always mean by heart what s/he speaks in words. Every boss knows that s/he is worth nothing without his/her team's support. In this world of growing competition in the market, and the race to success and growth to achieve one's professional goals; building a robust team is of prime importance. Every good boss will always keep a balance of pressure and pad.

Every boss has a single objective in mind when they scold, shout, drive, ignore or are aggressive with you; that is, 'to get the best out of you'. Such pressures are bound to come your way in such a high-paced race to success and recognition. As long as it is professional it is always good for you; but if it starts getting personal, the time has come for a change of boss. Before you take this call, keep in mind that there is something called 'management of your boss'. Read along to equip yourself with this powerful tool.

Everything that happens to you happens because of you. Before you discard your boss, there is always an opportunity for you to look at yourself on what you have been doing and what you have not, to keep your boss happy. You will never have a choice to pick your boss and as a professional you should never be dependent on one boss unless you are just doing a job and not working towards building your career. We are not saying you need to bend over backwards to please your boss, certainly not; but then there are certain things that you must keep in mind to keep your boss happy.

Every person has certain expectations from his/her colleagues and team members. Everyone wants to work with dependable and dedicated team members. Your boss knows that there's no point constantly changing people in the team and to keep testing for new candidates. And, in the long run it is a sheer waste of time and will slow down the pace of growth and key deliverables. If attrition under a certain boss is high, s/he has to look inward to figure out if the reason is him/herself. Is the boss causing the damage? Every boss would have expectations like a normal human being and a good professional. In today's corporate world, professionals are executives and not clerks, because they are paid to handle attitudes. They are expected to handle tough situations as well as their key deliverables. You cannot, at most times, change the situation around you; but you can mould yourself to suit the situation around you. Success lies in this. You never had the choice to pick your parents, your brother/sisters, sons and daughters; but you make it a point to keep them happy, and most of the time you achieve this by changing yourself and catering to their expectations. You forever need to mould yourself to achieve better results. Similarly, this holds good with your professional life. You cannot pick your boss, but then you do realise that your boss, after all, is the source for your growth, success and happiness in life. If you are happy at office, you are excited at home. So, dedicate some time to mould yourself into a personality your boss would like.

**Prepare yourself**

Remember, the first objective of your relationship with your boss is work. The first and foremost thing to attempt and continuously strive for is to develop trust and dependability at work. If you are expecting this trust to develop on its own or without putting in work, then either you are naïve or are a recipient of favouritism from your boss. No boss will ever respect you without you being dependable at work. By work we mean what s/he has hired you for and the results expected from you.

**Role Clarity**

It is your boss's responsibility to clarify your role and expectations from you. If you are not clear and feel any ambiguity about your role, you have all the rights to clarify it with your boss and take guidance. You should not let any unspecified situation creep in, where you are asked to do something and you have been clueless that you are supposed to deliver it. Spend time in understanding your role and deliverables. Any role will have practical action on a daily basis. It is imperative to demand time from your boss to understand your role in complete clarity and do confirm your understanding about your role and what is expected of you. Even if you have to take extra time to clarify or you feel your boss is getting irritated sometimes, it is better to make your boss understand the importance of the exercise, for both you and your boss alike. There is no sense in doing anything without knowing whether it is per the company's objective or to support your boss's key deliverables. In fact, any good boss will understand this and should love to spend time to clarify issues and prepare their soldiers for the battlefield.

It is a one-time activity. Once your role is clarified, you are ready to start delivering as per role understanding, and your first step towards building a fruitful business relationship with your boss has begun.

### Keep the Boss Posted

Your boss will always be busy with the rest of their reportees and seniors. S/he might not have time for you unless you ask for it. It could also be vice versa; your boss could have all the time for you and be constantly at your back to get an update. Most of the time either s/he is calling you or meeting you to take an update or gathering information from you. If s/he is not, grab every opportunity to update him/her on regular important developments in your projects and work. Many bosses do not have time to go through long mails or cc-marked mails. Many a time they might not realise the importance of the mail content unless they are personally told about it in person or through SMS. Everyone reads SMSes.

Too many or too few updates are dangerous. Please make it a point that in case of any development, the first person to be updated is your boss. No one likes it if any unique information is withheld by you. Keep a balance of updates to your boss. Any crisis that you may face for closure, reasons for low-target achievements, serious complaints, and day or month achievements should be known to him/her. Put yourself in your boss's shoes. Wouldn't you like your team member to update you on time? So when your boss asks you, you should be ready with your instant update. This gives the impression that you have a good grip of the situation.

There will be many situations when your boss has given you work and s/he forgets about it. But, s/he will only forget momentarily, for some time, but will remember all of a sudden in one meeting and ask you for an update. If you fumble then, there goes your credibility with your boss. Remember, your boss will like to be kept updated even if s/he has forgotten about it temporarily. Make it a point to update your own work. By doing this, you are making him/her feel important and that you are taking his/her words with dedication and sincerity. This goes a long way in building credibility with your boss.

Even on the personal front, if you feel that there are any new developments, either good or bad, which might affect your work tomorrow, it is better to keep him/her posted. Just be ready for any emergency leave. No boss likes unplanned leaves. If s/he is aware of the situation, s/he will understand your situation and bear with you rather than making a bad impression. Moreover, s/he will not display displeasure regarding your unplanned leave to other team members.

### Walk in and out for Advice and Guidance

This is an extremely effective way of making anyone feel important. If you are asking for guidance, you are already telling him/her about your faith and respect for his/her knowledge. And, any human being will like it. Do grab every opportunity to take guidance or advice over anything from your boss. Looking for advice does not mean that if you are stuck on something that you should just go and sit in front of your boss! Do apply your mind to how you could work around, what can be done and what the options are, as per the best of your ability and place those options in front of your boss. No boss likes to listen to only problems, especially if you haven't applied your mind at all. But, s/he loves to be given the options you have worked on and then provide solutions.

## Don't Let your Boss Down

Your professional environment leaves you in the same atmosphere as your boss. Do not let any situation arise where your boss has had to cut a sorry figure because of you. On the professional front, many projects and tasks are imposed on you even if you feel it is not worth spending time on it. Someone in the organisation would have had a bright thought and it might happen that it lands on your boss for execution, whether your boss believes in it or not. You have to gel with the situation whether it is imposed on you or even if you are doing it at your will. If it has to be done anyway, you might as well do it with complete sincerity and reach a conclusion.

Always support your boss with tactics in tough situations. You could have an argument over some issue with your boss in a closed room. But do not show denial in front of other functions/departments. It is not good to leave your boss alone during an argument or discussion in front of others. Go ahead with your boss, supporting him/her, providing data to enhance the chances of winning the debate/argument. Show complete solidarity and support. And, it should not be out of self-interest. What s/he does for you stands true for him/her as well. After all, your boss is in the same race as you are in, for growth and success.

It is needless to mention that breaking any office rules and regulations, fudging with financials, attitude problems, manipulation of data or low performance will let your boss down more than you. If any manipulation has been done without your consent, you can deny it and clarify your stand immediately.

### What your Boss Likes and Dislikes

Do analyse the behaviour of your boss off and on and mould yourself accordingly. There are some bosses who do not like to be disturbed too often and some who like to spend time alone in the morning to start their day. You should always make a note of things which upset them the most, it may be discipline, too many mails, over-friendliness, unnecessary laughs, coming too close to them without wishing them and even unnecessary flattery, disturbance on weekends, sharing dirty jokes, etc. It could be vice versa also. You are expected to deal with him/her accordingly. Keep a close watch for a while and you will be able to gauge what your boss likes or dislikes.

It is better to know what s/he likes the most on the professional front. One thing that all bosses dislike are 'reminders'. Either reminders to you to complete your task, or receiving reminders from others because you have not completed your task. This we can mention without any doubt, is the foremost professional aspect of dislike by any boss. Many bosses like to be called by their first name and many still expect to be called 'Sir' or 'Ma'am'. Some would expect you to show respect by standing up whenever s/he is at your desk, some may find it totally unnecessary. It is imperative for you to understand what ticks and what doesn't with your boss. It is important to know his/her hobbies and interests. You can always find an opportunity to talk about his/her hobbies and update him/her on these interests. Any foodie boss would like to know about new eating joints and specialty restaurants. You may use this opportunity to build a rapport based on things other than work. When you are talking to any person on a topic other than work at a workplace, it means you are initiating and building a rapport other than work. You have to find an opportunity to spend some easy and light times with your boss, but as per his/her will, not yours.

You can also get to know about preferences from the accessories and cabin of your boss – family photos, books, trophies, watch, pen, etc. But do remember, your objective is only to build a good rapport, not to take extra advantage out of this. Your relationship is of work and that should be your priority and should be complete in every aspect before you find your place in his/her space. It is upto him/her, to invite you in to his/her space and not your will to go without invitation. And, it takes time so have patience, if you are fulfilling your first objective of work, you will find a place for sure.

**What your Boss Expects from you**

Apart from what we have discussed till now, your boss expects loyalty from you. The boss wants people who will always be by their side and support them in crisis and tough situations. Remember, you will always be tested in tough times and you have to show your loyalty in those situations. Sitting late in office during a crisis, working on weekends without complaining and offering to go beyond your area of delivery, touring regularly, is a step towards showing your loyalty towards him/her.

It is important to go beyond your call of duty. Even if your particular function is not going through a crisis but another one of your boss's functions is, please do make an effort to do whatever is in your capacity to get the situation under control. This solidarity will go a long way in winning your boss's confidence. Always ask your boss if there is anything more you can do, besides what you have already been doing. Talk to your boss about your performance and if there is any way you can improve it further to suit his/her standards. Mention that you would like to improve your performance further and seek guidance on how to go about it. Come up with pleasant surprises for your boss, by providing some solid inferences with your data, or plans on cutting costs, or anything that will enhance your deliveries even further. Do not wait for your boss to tell you to do that. Do it proactively. Constantly innovate new ideas in your area and present it to your boss.

Everyone expects honesty, and no wonder it is a best policy. You should always try not to fall into any situation where you have to lie to your boss. Be honest in your dealings and there is no reason to make a fool of him/her by telling a lie. Only one such situation will take your impression away for life. During your entire office hours, your boss should know what you are doing and about your whereabouts.

Another thing all bosses expect is discipline and punctuality. Your boss might be too soft to tell you harshly about the concern over your late arrival to office or any other kind of indiscipline. But, take it from us, no boss likes it. You may be working late sometimes, but that doesn't give you the prerogative of coming late the next day, unless your boss proactively tells you to.

The boss expects you to give genuine views about anyone and in the best polite way. S/he does not expect you to gossip about other members of the team unless s/he is asking for it. Give honest feedback about surroundings and without mincing words. If you do not know about the person, refuse to give feedback. Do not think that your boss will like if you are giving diplomatic and self-made feedback and opinion. If you have to provide an opinion about the personal life of someone without your will, ensure you refuse, because, that's honesty again. But then again, there are some bosses with who you may be otherwise very friendly, in which case it is at your discretion to share or not to share personal details.

Likewise, your boss expects you not to gossip about him/her with other functions. Whether you like your boss personally or not is beside the point. Your growth in the organisation and your career will shine only if you maintain a cordial relationship with your boss, as s/he is the person who is going to recognise you and guide you to achieve higher goals. So, there's no point bringing in animosity between you both. A smart worker would work with the boss rather than against!

Ensure all targets and tasks are achieved as planned. But, what your boss wants to see foremost is the amount of effort you have made to achieve your goal. He expects you to make your best effort to complete your tasks. At the end of it, if you are short of your target by a small margin, your boss will forgive you. But, your efforts must be sincere and your boss should view it like that. If you can achieve that, you are home safe!

## Learn to say 'no' to your Boss

If you do not want to be known as a 'Yes boss' champ, you better learn to say 'No boss' for what is not acceptable to you. This is true for targets, projects, weekend working, etc. And, if you find your boss is egoistic about this, do not fall into an argument. But, do discuss it. Discussions can lead to conclusions, but not arguments. You can never win an argument with your boss. If you win an argument with your boss, you will have lost many other more impacting and career-defining things. So, it is always better to lose an argument and win the rest of it. What we are trying to tell you here is that you needn't be submissive and be a 'yes man'. State your point of view if you disagree. You may not hold on to your point of view, if it seems to be destructive in a way that it might lead to an argument, but you must state it! Let your boss know softly, that you have agreed to do it but you do not personally subscribe to it. You are expected to handle the situation and gel with it. But, if you do find a suitable situation later, do discuss it with your boss (without sounding too insistent and rigid) and close the issue.

Too much of 'Yes boss' is again not appreciated by many bosses. They would rather work with a team that has a point of view, a thinking team rather than a robotic and clerical one. You will be taken for granted for sure, if you keep accepting whatever comes your way. At times they would like to be confronted and be reassured that you have a rock solid head on your shoulders.

**Conflict with your Boss**

The most sensitive situation of your career is when you have a conflict with your boss. This is the worst situation for any professional at any level. We do not wish this situation even for our enemies (though neither of us have any). The first thought when something like this happens is that you would want to quit. That is an option no doubt, but how are you sure that you will not find a similar boss in your next job? There is no guarantee on that. So, as the saying goes 'A known devil is better than an unknown devil'. Your first thought should be to work around the matter with your current boss. The conflicts may be of two kinds, personal and psychological or purely professional. The latter is easier to deal with than the first kind. The first one may arise out of very sensitive factors like the boss is threatened by you because you may be much better than him/her, in your personality and your popularity.

A professional conflict can arise either out of your non-performance or excessively high expectations from your boss. It is wise to have differences with your boss on a professional front in some situations, but not all. But, the day it turns personal, it becomes a serious conflict. Mostly, such conflicts are silent and keep magnifying within. So, in either situation, the ideal way to go about it is to have a one-on-one discussion. Don't just go and sit in front of your boss and say you have a problem. Be prepared. That is the key. Make a list of all the things that according to you have caused all the conflict and how you view it. This can be the starting point of your discussion. Also, carry with you instances when you have had conflicts and what your thoughts are on it. If it's a personal issue, then it can be a subjective discussion and there are no guarantees where it might lead. But, if it is a professional conflict, it can be stated in points where you both differ in your views and how you can reach a point of mutual consent. Do not hesitate to tell your boss that you find the targets too high, and explain why you think it is impossible to ride on these targets, or if you find a project is not worth the time and effort you are spending on it, etc. Give valid reasons and explanation. Keep your fingers crossed that your boss is sensible enough to see your reasoning. If s/he thinks you are in the wrong, let him/

her point out to you where you can make amends and be ever willing to accept ANY criticism without defending yourself, even if you have solid points to defend yourself. Do it at the end of your boss's speech to you.

If you lose your temper, you will never get the credit, neither can you win. You have to mould yourself in the way that s/he wants you to work. If s/he only expects you to work as per his/her direction, mould yourself and go with the flow. Some give you freedom to work and perform and some want to get the job done as per direction. Both have pros and cons. Freedom at work is like a rope, you can use it like a ladder and climb up or with the same rope you can be hanged.

You should build confidence to discuss anything that is upsetting you or that you are not comfortable with with your boss. If you get a feeling that your boss is overdoing his/her act with you in certain situations, do ensure to take it up with him/her, politely but firmly. There is no other way to resolve issues with the boss; either you do what you have been asked to do or you have the choice to speak it out with him/her. And, if you think you are not able to reach any conclusion, change your boss before you spoil your relation with him/her beyond repair. Never tell your boss that you are quitting because of him/her. The corporate world is very small and there is no guarantee that you will not come face-to-face with that person ever again!

In fact, whenever you quit an organisation, quit positively. Don't leave any bad taste and definitely do not burn bridges.

### Delight your Boss

By now, in your work front, you have already done well enough to keep your boss satisfied with your performance. Delighting your boss includes extending courtesies to make him/her feel special, respected and important.

The boss expects that his/her team should give him/her credit for success. Any opportunity to compliment your boss should not be missed. 'This is only because of you', 'the credit goes to you, boss' and other such phrases will delight your boss. Whenever there is success the boss is expected to reward and recognise good work, but the boss usually gets left behind in this. So, a team member attributing his/her success to the boss is very welcome! This can also be reiterated in day-to-day conversations by using phrases like 'as you wanted', 'as you said', 'what you said was right', 'your idea is good', 'what you are saying is correct', etc. These phrases should be used by you liberally while conversing with your boss.

Respect the privacy of your boss, leave his/her office space if s/he is attending to a personal call. Do not show too much interest to stare at the laptop screen or any other papers in his/her room without consent, even in his/her absence.

Give honest compliments to your boss. Whenever you like any gesture, appearance, accessories, etc., find an opportunity to mention it. Do it well; it should never sound like flattery.

Your boss's mails in your inbox are most important and should get utmost priority – 100 per cent response within the same day is mandatory. Please reply even if you are not ready with the answer to what is asked for. Do write that you will update them later, with a timeline. And, stick by the timeline.

Keep a check-list in your diary, of the tasks entrusted by your boss. Make best use of mail features to highlight and follow-up important mails of your boss. Never forward a mail to a boss without any comment. Always mention a snapshot of the trailing mail with a comment about what is expected out of them. Your boss's name should always be first, whether s/he is marked 'To' or 'cc'.

In a meeting, if your boss has made the wrong update, do not correct him/her in the open. Do find a way to update him/her silently later, by SMS; or whisper if s/he is sitting beside you. Delight him/her by making all arrangements for a meeting if s/he has called for one.

Organising a special room for your boss during travel and taking extra care for their stay is always a delight for every boss.

Remembering and wishing them on their birthday and anniversary is a must. Take an initiative in getting flowers, cake, card, etc., and get the card signed by the team members and organise a gift with a contribution. Avoid giving personal and individual gifts to your boss, unless you are good friends otherwise. Do decorate his/her cabin. In the event of an anniversary, you can send flowers at home. Commenting to your boss, a week or two in advance, on his/her upcoming birthday will be taken in good spirit and will be delightful.

After you, your boss is the most important person in your office. S/he decides your present and future. Corporate also works on a certain hierarchical system. Your boss will only talk to his/her peers and spread good words about you. And, your boss's peers are all your seniors. You have to respect this person the way s/he is. This identity in corporate life can easily either disturb your personal life or make your career prosper. S/he can easily take your happiness away even at home, or ensure happiness for years.

A good boss builds your personality and demonstrates skills to make you a good personality. S/he shares his/her experiences and knowledge to teach and develop you as a tough professional and a good person. Bosses do not want you to make the same mistakes which they themselves have learnt through trial and error. Your boss can impart knowledge and the skill required for your job. What s/he cannot teach or imbibe in you is dedication and sincerity to your job. There are some basic values which make a solid foundation for your character and make an impact on people around you. Let's take it up in the next session!

‘Hundred per cent of anything is not possible, even truth.’

# Session X

# THINGS THAT MAKE AN INSTANT IMPACT

There are some aspects that add an instant impact to your personality and to your attitude some of which we have mentioned below. It's not possible, rather not required for all to be covered instance by instance, because from whatever we have covered here, it should give you a ballpark idea of what kind of things make this instant impact.

This session is going to be one with several examples, because like we mentioned earlier, there are some things that only narration of real world instances would do justice.

This is one area where there has been immense learning for us as professionals. There are some things we do innocently and unintentionally, but that can be complete turn-offs. It might put off someone so badly that the entire impression of you would be destroyed. We would like you to pay a lot of attention to what we will mention in this session. To some of you it might seem very basic; however, it's always good to get your basics right so that the foundation is strong and what you build on that can withstand any pressure or any growth.

**Understand Other People**

Let us start the session by giving you an example of one of our colleagues. Some things cannot be written in the form of 'dos and don'ts'. Because the situations are so delicate and diverse, they cannot be put into definitive words. Instances would give you a chance to judge for yourself what's acceptable and what's not. This gentleman, our colleague, is a very committed worker, genuinely interested in doing his job well, who comes up with some brilliant ideas, is an asset to have around in the team, and is also a good human being. But, he doesn't manage to lead his team effectively, he doesn't manage to garner their respect and fails to appear intelligent and attractive to his peers, colleagues and seniors. You might think if he's that good at his work and a good human being too, then why is this so?

We have known this gentleman closely. We've seen his boss go through a tough time with his seniors, trying to prove to them that he's indeed efficient; as well as the colleague's team, who come and crib to his boss, that he's indeed a nice guy, if you can only look beyond his mannerisms and communication. But, one hard fact of this corporate life is that no one really has enough time and no one is really willing to put in that energy to understand the kind of person you are. What they see is what they believe. Another hard fact is, once a perception is built it is almost unshakeable, unless you work very hard to break that, for which you may not really have the luxury of time; all of us have enough and more work at our desks or out in the field at any point of time.

As you'd have gathered by now, we did have a fondness for this gentleman. Being his close colleagues we got to see numerous sides of him, as a worker, as a manager, as a father, as a husband, as a son and so on. However, there were times when either of us were extremely busy with someone in our cabin and he would just come by and stand in front of the glass cabin because he thought he had something very urgent or important to discuss. At times he would also gesture towards us to open the door and almost barge in. It not only distracts the current meeting, but would also put a pressure on us to finish it fast, whether or not one has actually come to a good conclusion. And, that would leave us perturbed. What one would have ideally liked him to do is to come outside the door once, show his presence and go back to his seat and come back to check some time later. If it was extremely urgent, one would expect him to send an SMS mentioning why he'd come and the criticality of the situation. This gives the other person a chance to judge if the current meeting was less critical than what he had in store for us, and would have made a decision accordingly.

Then there were times when he would be extremely agitated with some fellow departments for good reason. But, the way he portrayed his irritation wouldn't help an inch towards an amicable solution. He would point a finger at his fellow peer's intent and write mails with all of what has been mentioned as a strict 'no' in our first chapter. Not only that, he would rush in to the cabin (no lurking around outside this time) scratching his head and other areas. Mind you, this wasn't intentional at all, and it was only because this poor fellow had been pushed to the corner and was a very agitated and anxious person. But, the rest of the world will not look at it like that. He will be ridiculed and worse still, though he is right, his better mannered and polite colleague may win over the situation, in all likelihood. Such is the damage you will cause to yourself, if these basics skip your mind. However difficult your situation, however tough your battle, there are some basic mannerisms and etiquette one must never ever overlook.

There is this other equally sweet fellow in office. However, he lacks the basics. One day on the way to the lift to go home, we saw this man running after his boss, calling out her name. She stopped to look. And, it turned out that he was running after her to tell her that he just got a call from this 'very big school' that his son's admission is through. She was the first person he wanted to break the news to. There were others waiting for the lift as well, and everyone looked at each other and there were varied emotions written large on their faces. Sycophancy is what comes to mind immediately, right? But actually the fact is that he had been with her since the time he was a junior employee. So, he held her in very high regard. But, even she was embarrassed with this whole situation. So, what do you suppose would have been a more appreciable thing to do? When you see that your boss is walking out to go home, instead of running after her and making a fool of yourself and creating a scene, use the good old phone. The thing to learn from this is, no matter how excited you are, how happy your heart is, you are in a formal work environment, and the basics need to be kept in mind.

### Take Genuine Interest

Either you go to people or people come to you, but show your natural and honest interest in people while meeting. You generally show your interest by eye-to-eye contact, with a genuine smile and expression on your face, actively listening to what the other person is saying. You can prove you are actively listening by asking relevant questions. We promise you, if you are listening with attention you will have a genuine expression and the right questions to ask. If your colleague has shared with you that his son is not well or his mother was hospitalised, you may like to probe further to know more details and even advise the colleague if you think you can. Enquiring after the same a few days down the line by meeting or texting about his/her son or mother's well-being is an example of genuine interest. And, be genuine at all levels of hierarchy in the organisation, whether it is with your boss or even the office boy who serves you tea or cleans your table.

### Dealing with a Situation of Panic

The last thing you ought to do is lose your cool. You may not be in a position to take control of the situation, but please don't be instrumental in making it seem larger than it actually is. The least you could do is make it seem smaller and pacify any colleagues who are hypersensitive. Be a part of the solution and not a part of the problem.

**Littering**

There was this instance we faced one day and our impression of that person no doubt has been damaged to a large extent. Littering. It's trivial yes, but very impacting. It shows clearly how conscious a person you are. There are no fines for littering in India. However, as grown adults we must have our own rules too. We had been for an outing with colleagues one day. We had some wafers and soft drinks and we were carrying all the empty cans looking for a place to dispose them off. Suddenly this man finished his drink and dropped off the can right where he was and continued to walk as if nothing happened. He had some wafers left in his packet and he offered it to us. We refused. He polished off the packet in a jiffy and he chucked the packet exactly the same way and carried on with his walk. That's not all. He noticed us holding on to our empty cans and packets and he suggested that we chuck them as well, and in fact said something like 'Why are you guys holding on to empty cans and packets?' Whew! There went our impression of this man, who we otherwise thought was really nice.

There's another instance on littering we would like to share. This gentleman was sitting in a meeting and involved in a critical discussion and was trying to change some policies, etc. There he was fiddling with his set of papers. But, he didn't stop at that. Unconsciously he was ripping off the paper, crumpling them into little balls and chucking them on the floor with great force, till somebody pointed it out to him. He was indeed very apologetic and picked up the paper balls and put them where they belonged, into the dustbin. So, you see we sometimes tend to do things that we are apologetic about later, but most of the time, the damage is already done.

Believe us, it's not such a big deal to keep in mind some of these basics that we will point out now. Develop these as a habit, a part of your being, don't merely memorise them as requirements for the corporate world.

## Eating with your Fingers

Try and avoid it during a high-end corporate lunch or dinner, but when you are generally out for a casual day-to-day meal with your colleagues, eating with your fingers is quite acceptable in India. Our cuisine is such that it tastes better when mixed with fingers. However, please keep in mind that you must eat with your fingers ONLY and not your entire palm. You can eat with poise. Just remember, only your fingers should have any food stuck to it and only that side of your fingers that is touching the food. Not the back of your fingers or your palm. And if you are say, eating rice, sometimes some rice tends to get stuck between our fingers and we have this habit of shaking that onto our plates. Please don't do that! Another thing to keep in mind is how you put the food in your mouth. Just take the food up to your mouth and push the contents with your thumb. Do not put all your fingers inside your mouth, and also avoid throwing food into your mouth from a distance. Do not make small bite size balls of your rice and curry, and line them up on your plate to put them into your mouth one by one. Mix just enough (with your fingers only, not your palm) for a couple of bites and then mix again. If you are used to eating any other way, it might take a bit of effort and time before you could get used to this; but let us tell you, it is worth it. While you are trying this out, you might think that you never got the taste of the food you were eating, because you were trying so hard to imbibe these basics! It's so much more worthwhile to sacrifice on the taste and comfort of eating for a few meals, if it gives you a lifetime supply of good food, right? Your *paapi pet* will be well taken care of as you steadily climb up the ladder.

## Getting too Physical

Getting too physical is like hitting a colleague really hard on the back or a casual slap on the backside, holding hands or keeping your arm around his/her shoulder (s/he might not mind as you actually may be close friends too, but the rest of the world will not look at it like that – they would find it rather sloppy and slouchy). Even going out of the way to wish someone a 'good day' may be out of place. Let us give you an example of this man in office. He holds quite a senior position in the company. At least once a day, this gentleman would be lurking around outside a cabin just to say 'good morning/afternoon/evening' if he got a chance to peep his head inside. You would think, oh that's all right, he means no harm! Yes you are right; he means no harm to anyone, but the harm he's causing himself by doing this is almost irreparable. The juniors do not respect him; his peers make fun of him. Not only that, there are some who take the liberty to sympathise with any person for having to tolerate him and some others tend to crack a joke or two. Now the least that one could gather from all of this is that he is being noticed and not in a positive way. Though it's a very passive action, people still notice if you are out of line.

Here we have tried our best to outline some of the things that you should avoid by all means. It may sound very basic again, but then sometimes unconsciously we get around to displaying just that. And, we have noticed that it is by habit that a person does most of the things mentioned below. It is hardly intentional. So, you have to be extra careful to avoid doing it, as it might just come to you naturally!

### Basic Things to Keep in Mind

**Putting your finger in your mouth to get at something stuck between your teeth** – Avoid this as much as possible. However, if it is painful, you may excuse yourself and head towards the restroom to get it out. However, if you are in a position where you are stuck and cannot get out, cover your mouth with one palm and use a toothpick with the other hand to get it out. After successfully getting it out, please do not chew on it. Just gulp it down with water immediately.

**Burping/Passing Gas** – You cannot be caught burping in a corporate atmosphere, or for that matter in any group.

**Switch off lights** – Do this when you are leaving a room. If there is an individual AC then switch that off too. Please do switch off the fan of a lift when you are stepping out.

**Blowing your nose/cleaning your eyes** – If you have to blow your nose, the restroom is the best option. In case that's not available, please use a tissue to blow only so much so that you get some immediate relief. Please do not blow your nose like you would in a restroom, over the wash basin. As soon as you can land yourself in a restroom, do so!

**Digging your nose** – This is by no means acceptable, however uncomfortable you might be. You necessarily need to find a restroom as early as possible.

**Digging into your ears** – Absolute no-no!

**Scratching your head for dandruff or your beard** – Not at all – scratching anywhere is forbidden for that matter!

**Cover your mouth with tissue while coughing** – Please make sure to carry some napkin or tissues if you have been coughing. Apart from spreading the infection to all your other colleagues, you will also quickly be the most undesirable person anyone would want to hang around with. Take care of your health and that of your colleagues as well.

**Spitting while talking** – This is a habit that's uncontrollable. You automatically tend to spit out sometimes, when you are talking excitedly or you have an animated discussion. Some people of course do not need excitement or animated discussion, they spit when they speak normally too. The best advice would be to see a doctor and find out why that happens. It could be the diet or any other reason. Sometimes when you are eating and talking at the same time, you might suddenly spit out food and that might land on your bosses' plate – that too, one month prior to your appraisal period. Think about that!

**Bad breath** – One should never take a chance to analyse whether or not his/her breath stinks. You could just openly ask your family or close friends. And, as soon as you get the feedback that it does, please make all necessary changes in your life immediately. Your diet, your personal mouth hygiene and whatever is the cause of your bad breath. Chew gum or pop in a mouth freshener every now and then to make sure your mouth doesn't smell.

Nicotine stains on teeth needs to be taken care of regularly. And if you are in the habit of chewing tobacco, consume very little quantities in office, as it emits an unbearable stink to the others. Also, it is a habit that is best avoided. So if you can, do give it up.

**Foul body smell** – Take immediate precautions to avoid body smell. This has been covered in detail in the session 'Appearance'.

**Hands** – Your hands must be kept very clean. Wash them regularly. Keep your nails trimmed and the edges cut well. Take an old tooth brush and brush your nails while having a bath. Both finger and toenails. Every single day.

Now we would like to take you through some of the positive attributes that you may want to imbibe. If you do, we can assure you, you will leave a really cool impression. Read through it thoroughly.

## Always Smile

It costs you nothing – but gives a lot back to you. When you cross each other along the corridor, or meet in the boardroom, or even in the restroom, flash a smile. Make sure when you smile your eyes smile too. Maintain eye contact. There is nothing worse than a fake smile. Everybody has the instinct to make out a fake smile from a real one. So smile and smile genuinely. It not only makes you seem to be a very approachable, pleasant, nice and friendly person, but let us tell you a secret; it also makes you seem more energetic. And, please do remove that frown, if you have one!

### Appear Energetic

This brings us to yet another of those things that will make an instant impact. Always look energetic. The way to do it is to smile. That's the first and foremost thing. Walk fast and in a crisp manner. A limp walk is a sure giveaway. Crack a few jokes. Yes you need not really do extensive and intensive work to seem energetic. In fact, should you be so tired, try and take up the intensive grilling assignments for the next day, if your work permits you. When you are tired the chances of error are almost doubled. Also, you may not be able to think your best.

### Appear Positive at all Times

Even during a casual conversation with your boss, never list down your road blocks and crib and complain about how much you are suffering. Talk about the positive things that you are up to and if you have to mention your roadblocks, mention it in the way of a solution that you have thought about and you seek his/her opinion on the same. Never ever complain about your colleagues in front of your boss. It doesn't help you build that reputation you are trying so hard to build. If your boss or a colleague proactively asks you about the problems you are facing, even then you can put it through to them in a very positive way. Mention it to them in a way that, though you are able to achieve your targets more or less, you could however do with a little extra support and guidance to overcome your problems. Instead of saying 'I have a problem at hand' you may try saying 'I have a situation at hand'. There may be times you will be asked to do something which you might not readily be available to do or the assignment might be out of your area of work or you may not be aware of it. Whatever the case may be, please do not start off your conversation with a 'no', or any negative connotation. It helps to tell the person when and how you will be able to assist or support, e.g. if a colleague comes asking for data which you do not maintain, you may approach it like this, 'This data that you are asking for is with so and so. Let's go and ask him/her for it.' And then accompany the person there, or at least make a call to the other person who has the data and inform him/her about the requirement or you may say, 'I am not the right person to get this job done. However, so and so is an expert in this area, let's approach him/her.' Once a requirement comes to you, treat it as your own, till you are able to place the person who came in with the request to the actual person who would be able to help.

**Solidarity**

Staying back with a colleague for a late night, even if you are not required to stay back, or coming on a holiday to keep your colleague company for a short while if s/he has to work, makes you adorable amongst your peers. Lending an ear to their problems and helping them with solutions is most desirable. Though you may not have immediate gains from doing this in terms of your performance, you will definitely gain in the long run. You will gain the trust and adulation from all, which you will definitely gain from in more ways than one.

## Talking Loudly and Angrily

You must avoid this to any extent possible. Let that emotion of yours be the last one to surface, in case of an argument or debate. We haven't said you must avoid it by all means (which actually would help no doubt) because there are times when it's just impossible to hold back. But, once we have mentioned it here as an undesirable attribute, whenever you succumb to this emotion, you will think about it later and it may help you have better control. Just because you are venting your anger you needn't talk loudly. And, if you must, please get into a room with the person you are angry with. Doing it in front of everyone, not only leaves a bad impression of you with the person you are shouting at, but also with all the bystanders. Your loss would be multifold. Whether you are right or wrong, acceptance levels of anger and loud outburst is very low.

## Appreciation and Compliments

Now this is very tricky indeed. Yes, most people love to be complimented. There is no doubt about that. But the problem is that most people can also make out a false compliment from a genuine one. So, how do you place your compliments? This requires an acute sense of timing and relevance. You must not be seen as a person who never compliments anyone, but place your compliments with care. Usually a broad smile with raised eyebrows and a reassuring look is a good enough compliment for a PPT (PowerPoint) well-presented. If you have to speak, just saying, 'Your views on this topic were very interesting' or something very simple is more than enough.

We have found that keeping compliments short, crisp and to the point normally helps. Place your compliment and quickly go on to another topic. 'This dress suits you', 'where did you pick this lovely dress', 'you look good today', 'your presentation was superb', 'you hit the nail on the head' – these are some compliments we have hardly ever seen failing to create the intended impact. But, prolonging the compliment makes it lose its impact and the other person starts to doubt if you are saying it genuinely. Complimenting too often ought to be avoided. Your compliment should hold the depth of a heartfelt compliment. Similarly, when you receive a compliment, don't get too involved in it. Don't deny it or boast about it. Just flash a smile or say a mild 'thank you', and move on with whatever you were doing.

**Extra-Curricular Activities/Hobbies**

If you play a musical instrument, or sing, or dance well, have lots of jokes up your sleeve, write or recite poems, you must never lose an opportunity to showcase your skills. Frankly, amongst the hundreds of team members we remember all of them who have performed in the annual functions/celebrations. And, we remember the ones that get awards month after month – the top performers! So you see, even if you are working your way up to become a top performer but are not there yet, you can be recognised by the other skills that you possess. And, being recognised means, if there is a special project coming up, you might be the chosen one to lead the project. And that might be your ticket to the top performer slot. Besides, it's very encouraging for a boss to see the various skills that the team possesses. Your peers and seniors will definitely have a positive feeling towards you and you will also gain their respect. So, if opportunities present itself in front of you, go ahead, shed all your inhibitions and showcase your inherent or acquired talents.

### Active Listener

It's not enough to just be an attentive listener if you want to make an instant impact on the person you are in conversation with. Be an active listener. What we mean by 'active' is, you must not only listen attentively but also participate in the conversation. How do you do that? One way is to reiterate the points made by the other person every now and then. Empathise with the person to a point that s/he feels you can feel the pain or pleasure being felt by that person. Offer a word of caution if it warrants one (but here you run the risk of being prescriptive, so be cautious about that), or a word of encouragement. Summarise the discussion at the end of the conversation to ensure both of you are on the same page. Now, these things you must not overdo, or else the entire focus of being a listener would be lost. In these kinds of situations you will gain by being sincerely involved and interested in the conversation, then you will automatically know when to butt in. There are conversations and discussions that you might find utterly boring. If it is a professional discussion, you have to pay attention, this is just one of the things that you ought to put up with, in your professional life. If it is a personal discussion, and it doesn't interest you in the least, it's better to find an excuse out of the discussion in the beginning itself, than to find yourself listening, but not attentive or active. The former is not as harmful as the latter.

While we have spoken extensively about things that make an instant impact, there are a few virtues that we would like to take you through, that might not make an 'instant' impact, but if practised religiously over time, will have a lasting impact and a beneficial one!

## Age-old Virtues

Old is Gold as the saying goes. There are some age-old virtues, if adopted, that tend to have a very positive impact on your personality. Sometimes what happens is that, in a bid to acquire the style and the glamour of the corporate world and trying to inculcate all the 'Corporate Etiquette' which is more intriguing, we tend to forget some of the basic values. These are values that all of us have been taught by our parents, grandparents, teachers, guardians from a very tender age. However, as we grow up, we find more fascinating mannerisms and in a bid to inculcate them, we overlook these basic virtues. Allow us to take you through the same, in relation to the impact it will have of you in the corporate world.

### Punctuality

We have heard about this virtue since the time we have been able to make sense of what is being talked to us. It is not unwarranted. Though a simple virtue, this speaks a lot about you as a person. How much respect you have for your fellow human beings shines right through, with this simple yet very powerful and impacting virtue. Your seriousness about your job, discipline while doing your work, your sincerity towards the organisation that pays your salary, all of these get installed in the minds of your colleagues, especially your senior colleagues, by this simple gesture. So, if you take this lightly it may not be the factor that will make you lose your job or your promotion, but if followed, would definitely help in keeping your job and your promotion.

**Honesty**

Another simple virtue that has been preached to us since we were toddlers. There is no medicine like honesty. It can cure any mishaps or any misgivings that someone might have about you. No one in this world is perfect. Even your boss commits mistakes, more than you can imagine, so every human is prone to mistakes. There would be many times you might find yourself in a messy situation, a sticky situation, and you might be horrified and may spend many sleepless nights trying to undo your situation, or some silly mistake. Let us assure you, there is absolutely no merit in trying to undo it. It almost never gets undone. The key is to admit it. And, while admitting the other person may have 'n' number of things to point out to you, instead of trying to defend yourself, practise yet another simple virtue, humility. Listen quietly. Though humility does not always work in your favour in the corporate world, in this situation it works wonders.

## Humility

Since we have stumbled upon this virtue, let us elaborate the use of this simple virtue made complicated by the workings of the corporate world. Practising this virtue is not as simple as 'punctuality' and 'honesty'. You have to exercise caution and some thinking before you practise this. What is it that you need to be cautious of, and how should you adopt humility? It is indeed distressing but true that being overly humble is sometimes taken as a sign of 'not being too knowledgeable on the subject', or 'a person with no opinion whatsoever, hence not intelligent enough' or even seen as 'being happy to be a doormat'. So, while being humble is respected, you must put forward your opinion, not in a conflicting kind of way, put forth politely but surely, e.g. you may start with 'I totally agree with you; however do you suppose we could look at this angle as well'. This way you have the other person feeling good about the fact that you appreciate what s/he is saying, at the same time you have put forward what you think on the subject as well. The best way is to let the other person speak whatever they have in mind, by not interrupting (even if you sometimes cannot control the urge of blurting out something that is totally in tangent) and then you slowly introduce your point of view.

## Sincerity

This attribute should shine through every small assignment you take up. Yes your bosses can normally see through your efforts. Even if your data doesn't speak of a frog leap in terms of your performance, the boss sees through to the hard work and effort that you have put in. And, more often than not, that is what the boss usually desires. There are so many other conditions that may affect your performance – market conditions, technical snags, support from other teams and more such. However, your efforts to overcome all of that must be completely sincere. Make sure you do not start your reviews with the reasons for your non-delivery. That's a killer. First you must mention what you have been able to achieve, and then when you talk about the road blocks, you must also put forth the solutions that you think could work best to overcome those. Then mention that you could do with some advice and guidance and support from your seniors to help you see it through. That's how you must always portray yourself.

**Assertive and not Aggressive**

There is a very thin line between these two attributes; however the positive or negative impact that it can create is huge. So, one needs to be extra cautious while trying to drive home one's point of view. One needs to be assertive no doubt, else this humility issue will get you; but being aggressive is not the solution. So, where do you draw the line? While putting across your point of view, if you are a bit pushy, self-assured, confident and firm, you will be seen as assertive. However, if you get hostile, violent (in the words that you use), destructive and insistent, your behaviour will be seen as aggressive, which is not such a pleasant trait to have. So, like we have mentioned above in the humility section, the best way is to let the other person complete what they are saying, till everything has been spoken out. Then you agree to the point of view, but put across your opinion as well. If you cannot reach a conclusion immediately, postpone the discussion; agree to disagree for the time being. That's the best way to part. Using sarcasm is the worst you could do, so avoid that by all means.

## Avoiding Sarcasm

Please note that there is a difference between being assertive and being rude and sarcastic. Some professionals feel that being sarcastic and being rude in public, humiliating others with personal remarks is an easy way to get a job done but not realising it is only CHEAP. It is easy for any senior to be rude or sarcastic towards the juniors; but one must keep in mind, only a happy person will deliver happy results. Seniors are expected to grow up to their levels and behave. Sarcasm is never a long-term grace; you tend to lose very early in your career graph.

## Politics

You would have come across this word many times so far in your life, even if you are a student yet to pass out of college. This is one virus that is available wherever there is power and relationship. This is a most dreaded virus but you just cannot avoid this. So just be ready and know that you will come across this everywhere you go. Politics cannot spread in any organisation without the support of seniors in power. In any organisation, it only starts at the top and flows down. You do not have to be part of politics to grow career wise, but you have to understand politics in your organisation for sure. It helps you deal with some people smartly. Remember people who are jealous of you, always feel that you are better than them in every aspect. So, when they cannot compliment you, they can only back stab you or speak ill of you. The only thing you have to do is keep your boss posted on all the activities you are doing. If your boss happens to be playing games with you, skip a level and approach a higher authority, from time to time. If it's crossing limits, change your workplace or your role. In any case you are not learning anything worthwhile from your current boss. As we mentioned earlier, surveys says 80 per cent of people change their jobs because of their bosses. They are said to quit their 'managers' and not the 'organisation'.

Just keep a note of these people and avoid them, nor are they of your calibre and neither can they add any value to you and your work. Rather feel happy and proud that you are better than them.

**Golden Rule**

You do not have to play politics,
but you have to understand it for sure.

**Know your Gadgets**

Electronics gadgets play a significant role in our day-to-day life. Many of you might be reading this book as an e-book and even on the internet. And, the way technology is growing especially in the communications field, it is mandatory for each one of us to keep ourselves up-to-date with the latest devices, especially those that we use in our professional interactions. If you are wondering how this creates an impacting impression in the professional world, it can only be illustrated by live example if you have ever come across a situation like that.

Although, it is mandatory for any organisation to keep IT professionals to help and guide us to keep devices working, this in fact works to be a disadvantage for most of us. We become so dependent on IT and inadvertently it becomes a hindrance for us to learn. Can you imagine a situation, where your laptop is not compatible with the OHP (Overhead Projector), when you need to present a PPT to senior management, what would you do? If yours is the first presentation, then you could of course be ready with your projection. But, what if you have to present in the middle of a meeting and you are struggling with your laptop to fix it to the OHP? None of the seniors would mind your taking help of an IT professional till s/he comes but they would definitely mind that you made them wait. There could be two choices, either you will be ready in advance or you will learn to do it yourself. People present are certainly going to take home an opinion about you. If you are good at managing such situations, people might not notice instantly, but being consistent in such situations would certainly lead to creating a favourable impression. Let's list some of the situations to gauge and gain your confidence in handling electronic devices.

- You are in the middle of teleconferencing with your colleagues and seniors. And you have to put yourself on mute so as not to disturb the others, when they are talking. Do you know how to put yourself on mute and unmute with base phones or your mobile?
- You are in the middle of a video conference interview and you have been told by the interviewer that you are

not in the TV frame and s/he is not able to see you, but s/he can hear you. What do you do?

- You are working in a group on excel and analysing data together. What if you have to map common data of two different files in one and make a pivot table out of it?
- Your boss has received a file which is not compatible on his laptop and is asking for an option to change the formatting of the file. What do you do?
- Your colleague is working on a very important file and forgets to save it. Do you think you can help your colleague retrieve the file?
- You printer is not responding to your laptop. Can you troubleshoot?
- Your immediate senior is not able to connect GPRS on his mobile. Do you think s/he will walk down to you for help?

We are not expected to be complete IT professionals but it is wise to gain knowledge and develop confidence on software, networking and connecting devices. Be a master on basic troubleshooting for devices you have around you. Building expertise on these electronic devices will not only add to your overall impression but also increase your own efficiency in work without wasting time on depending on others to assist you.

Keeping in line with all devices is not going to be easy and will always be challenging. This is one area that is constantly evolving. We are dealing with technology at every point of time, whether it's your GPS system in your car, microwave at home, online check-in at the airport ... the list is endless. And it will continue to be so as time goes by.

Develop an interest in technology. If you have not undergone a basic computer course while you were a student, there is no harm attempting one now. Reading books on the computer will not help you learn. Software-based devices help you learn faster and are better coupled with practise. It is advisable to enrol yourself in a crash course on basic computer skills and networking.

Always attempt to resolve your problem yourself first. Even if you are not able to fix it yourself, you will definitely gain knowledge about other features of the devices and applications.

If you do need to ask for help, we suggest you work along with the IT person while s/he resolves your problem. This will help you understand what the problem was and how to resolve it. Also, next time, you will certainly be competent enough to resolve the same problem yourself and help others resolve it too.

Take an interest in educating yourself with new devices, new technology and services that you come across. If you happen to come across new features or services and you can't seem to use it, call up the related number to get the maximum information available.

Here one thing to remember and be extremely cautious about is not to use official resources like your desktop/laptop, telephone, fax machine, photocopiers, etc., for personal purposes. If you simply have to, please take permission before doing so. Don't ever 'get caught' doing it.

Another thing to remember is that official gadgets are office property. Be especially considerate while using common gadgets like photocopier, fax machine, common printer, etc. Ensure everybody gets a fair chance. Do not hog the entire machine without any consideration for the others. Always patiently stand in queue in case there is one. If you have a whole bunch of pages to be photocopied, allow your colleague standing behind with just a couple of pages to go ahead of you. If you are in a hurry or need something urgently, you may politely ask the person in front of you, whether it is okay to break the queue and explain the situation to him/her.

# AFTERWORD

So friends .... With this we have come to the end of the book and the beginning of your show! You must be thinking, this book has covered every possible situation you may face in your work environment, but is it really necessary to be so perfect? It's so difficult. It is necessary, if you wish to climb up the corporate ladder and see yourself at the tip of the pyramid sometime in life. Is it so tough? Well, not really. For those of you who wish to do it, you will find that everything is doable. But, then if you do not wish to do it, you will find even moving an inch in that direction very painful. While following every detail written in this book may sound formidable, if you really look deeper, you will see that not all of it is required to be done at one go. You just need to be alert in every situation and use the advice given to you in this book when you are faced with a particular situation, that's it. For those of you who want to achieve something in life, following these basic principles is a cakewalk. But then like we mentioned, for those of you who don't see value in it, moving every inch will be a huge effort.

We have tried our best to cover everything we think you would require to conquer all seasons of the Corporate World ... Summer ... Autumn ... Winter ... Spring! We hope to have empowered you enough to tackle the 'other side of the corporate world' ... the hidden side ... but one of the most impacting ones! We do confess that we wouldn't have covered EVERY POSSIBLE SITUATION. But, we have managed to give you a basic understanding, a foundation from which you can work. No two situations are similar, because it involves different people, different attitudes and different atmospheres, so it is almost impossible to cover every sort of personality and every atmosphere.

With this book, our objective is to create awareness and bring sensitivity to any situation or occurrences and equip you to take action accordingly. If you think that this book has given you even 10 per cent of something new, something you never thought of, and has ignited a thought and have made you act on it, we consider our effort (of writing this book) well worth it. If any of you feel that you were already aware of all of this and have been practising it on a day-to-day basis, then you are heading towards success at a much faster pace than your colleagues and subordinates. First, accept our compliments and good wishes, and second, please promote these virtues – by means of recommending this book, or by giving examples of your real-life situations during tea/coffee times, or giving one odd gyaan session to your teams on the necessity of it all. Please support us and spread this much-needed awareness.

Now that you are equipped, we pray you have been able

to implement most of it in your day-to-day life and are already beginning to see some changes in your behaviour and others' behaviour towards you. Now while you introspect at night, hopefully you will find that you have indeed been able to metamorphose yourself into a desirable person among your colleagues.

A good manager has to be a good human being as well; rather, he is only a good manager because he is a good human. Please remember the best compliment you can ever get in your life is being recognised as a good human being. Your growth is not only your happiness and pride, but also for your family and the organisation you work with. Your job satisfaction and timely career growth builds confidence and makes you a happy person by nature. Happy people spread happiness and happiness brings good health and good health is followed by wealth, respect, love, fame, success. What else you can ask for! This certainly seems like gyaan ... but, deep in our hearts we all know it is true.

Keep at it day after day and believe us ... all that is mentioned in this book will become your very nature ... and you will be able to sail through your corporate journey, climbing the ladder with elegance, with ease, as long as you follow these basic guidelines coupled with a great performance at work! We suggest you keep this book handy with you so you may check back every time you are faced with a trying situation.

Thank you for taking the initiative to read this book. This shows your seriousness and dedication to grow. We wish you success in all your future endeavours always and we want to be party to your success and growth and wish to begin our relationship with you. We promise to be there for you whenever you need us. We have opened up various channels for you to be able to communicate with us whenever you feel the need for advice from a more experienced friend. We would to like know your comments on our book, so we request you to join us on Facebook. We look forward to hearing your success story!

Best wishes always!

# INDEX